LINCOLN CHRISTIAN COLLEGE

W9-CBV-450

He Speaks to Me

He Speaks to Me

Preparing to Hear the Voice of God

PRISCILLA SHIRER

MOODY PUBLISHERS
CHICAGO

© 2006 by
PRISCILLA SHIRER

All rights reserved. No part of this book may be reproduced in any form without permission in writing from the publisher, except in the case of brief quotations embodied in critical articles or reviews.

All Scripture quotations, unless otherwise indicated, are taken from the *Holy Bible, New International Version*®. NIV®. Copyright © 1973, 1978, 1984 by International Bible Society. Used by permission of Zondervan Publishing House. All rights reserved.

Scripture quotations marked THE MESSAGE are from *The Message*, copyright © by Eugene H. Peterson 1993, 1994, 1995. Used by permission of NavPress Publishing Group.

Scripture quotations marked ESV are taken from *The Holy Bible, English Standard Version*. Copyright © 2000, 2001 by Crossway Bibles, a division of Good News Publishers. Used by permission. All rights reserved.

Scripture quotations marked NASB are taken from the *New American Standard Bible*®, Copyright © 1960, 1962, 1968, 1971, 1972, 1973, 1975, 1977, 1995 by The Lockman Foundation. Used by permission.

Scripture quotations marked CEV are taken from the *Contemporary English Version*. Copyright © 1991, 1992, 1995 by American Bible Society. Used by permission.

Scripture quotations marked NLT are taken from the *Holy Bible, New Living Translation*, copyright © 1996. Used by permission of Tyndale House Publishers, Inc., Wheaton, Illinois 60189. All rights reserved.

Scripture quotations marked NKJV are taken from the *New King James Version*. Copyright © 1982 by Thomas Nelson, Inc. Used by permission. All rights reserved.

Scripture quotations marked ASV are taken from the *American Standard Version*. Copyright © 1901 by Thomas Nelson & Sons, Copyright © 1929 by International Council of Religious Education. All rights reserved.

All italicized Scripture is the author's emphasis.

Cover Design: John Rodda
Cover Photo: Photodisc
Editors: Judith St. Pierre and Ali Childers

Library of Congress Cataloging-in-Publication Data

Shirer, Priscilla Evans.
    He speaks to me : preparing to hear the voice of God / Priscilla Shirer.
    p. cm.
    ISBN-13: 978-0-8024-5007-4
    1. Spiritual life--Christianity. 2. Hearing--Religious aspects--Christianity. I. Title.

BV4509.5.S49 2006

2005033175

ISBN: 0-8024-5007-5
ISBN-13: 978-0-8024-5007-4

We hope you enjoy this book from Moody Publishers. Our goal is to provide high-quality, thought-provoking books and products that connect truth to your real needs and challenges. For more information on other books and products written and produced from a biblical perspective, go to www.moodypublishers.com or write to:

Moody Publishers
820 N. LaSalle Boulevard
Chicago, IL 60610

1 3 5 7 9 10 8 6 4 2

Printed in the United States of America

11371/

Gratis

For Daddy
The one who gave me a passion to know Him and make Him known.

Contents

PART 3
A SET-APART HOLINESS

PART 4
A STILL ATTENTIVENESS

PART 5
A SOLD-OUT HUNGER

PART 6
A SERVANT SPIRIT

Very Special Thanks

To my sweet husband, Jerry: I was *surprised* that God called me into ministry ten years ago, but I am *astounded* at what God has done since He called us into ministry six years ago. Thank you for being my life partner in both marriage and ministry. Who would have guessed that God had this in mind for us?

To the Moody Publishers family: Thank you for the purity with which you serve the Master in your work. God does great things through you. I am so blessed to be serving with you to teach God's Word to God's women.

To my new friend, Judith: I am amazed! Thank you for making my thoughts palatable to readers. You've made it easy for them to digest the meaty biblical principles found in these pages. I hope we get to do it again soon!

Foreword

As I stared at the title to this book, I felt the emotion well in my throat. At the risk of sounding dramatic, I can't think of a spiritual reality that moves and astonishes me more on a daily basis than God's willingness to speak to us and give us ears to hear. I never get over feeling completely amazed any time something confirms that I really did hear God on a matter. To me, the whole process is miraculous. The first recorded words out of the mouth of God erupted a universe out of absolute nothingness. His words alter anything that truly hears them. You and I want to hear them. Discern them. Respond to them.

Communication is the essence of all relationships. Like most married couples, my husband, Keith, and I have very different personalities and ways of expressing ourselves. We've had to learn how to read one another and speak one another's "language." I remember days when my daughters would try to tell me something from one end of the house while I was in the other. So much lay between us— walls, radios, a blaring TV—that I could faintly hear their voices but I couldn't understand what they were saying. "Come closer so I can hear you better!" Without the ability to speak, hear, and respond, we'd never have experienced true family. The only thing interacting would have been our dirty clothes in the washer.

I'd heard of Priscilla Shirer for a year or two before I finally got to meet her face-to-face. I knew I was going to be impressed with her because I'd heard such wonderful things from people whose "taste" I trusted. Still, I was totally floored. Not only was she beautiful, articulate, and smart, she was warm and extremely likeable. I might have been jealous of Priscilla—she's so darling, wise, and young, after all—but her way so disarming I couldn't be anything but drawn to her. If you don't know her already, may I have the honor of introducing you to my little sister in Christ and my soul sister in the study of God's Word? Please meet Priscilla Shirer. Study with her, learn from her, and fall in love with her. This study won't be her last but, for starters, what topic could be more critical than learning to position ourselves to hear the voice of God and respond to it?

I can't wait to see what God's going to do with Priscilla. I'll be cheering her on all the way . . . while choking on the dust.

Go, girl. I'm nuts about you.

Beth Moore

Positioning Ourselves to Hear from God

While I was growing up, my grandmother always gave my older sister a box of clothes and shoes for Christmas. Every year a box arrived with Chrystal's name on it, and every year I watched her unpack all the goodies. Inside was the beautiful kind of clothes little girls used to wear—dresses with big frills at the bottom and patent leather shoes.

I didn't mind that the box was for my sister. In fact, I would get excited watching her unwrap everything because I knew that eventually she would outgrow it, and it would be mine. But something happened to me when I was about nine or ten. Suddenly when I watched Chrystal unwrap the box, I wasn't as happy anymore. I no longer wanted hand-me-downs. I wanted my own gift—one that had been picked out especially for me.

As believers, we oftentimes get used to and even become dependent upon hand-me-down revelations about God. We allow others to spoon-feed us the Word of God. But as you mature spiritually, don't you want God to send you a special gift-wrapped message with your name on it—for Him to reveal something very specific about your life? When that time comes, you need to know how to listen for His voice.

I believe that Scripture tells us how we can prepare ourselves to hear what God wants to say specifically to us. Please don't misunderstand. This isn't just some pie-in-the-sky religious issue. It's down-to-earth and intensely practical. When I began my study, the demands of life were threatening to overwhelm me. With a husband, two small children, and a ministry, I desperately needed to hear from God for instruction, guidance, and power. Yet I wasn't hearing from Him nearly enough.

The Lord doesn't speak in a whisper or in a dark corner somewhere where people can barely hear; nor does He try to trick us because He knows we can't understand what He's saying. "You are my witnesses," declares the Lord, "and my servant whom I have chosen, so that you may *know* and *believe* me and *understand* that I am he" (Isaiah 43:10). God doesn't have a case of cosmic laryngitis, and nothing is wrong with His transmitter. Our receiving equipment, however, often leaves a lot to be desired.

When I wasn't hearing from God, I got into the Bible for myself to find out how I could hear His voice more clearly. As I searched Scripture, I saw that God often spoke to people because they were prepared to hear from Him, and I realized that maybe He was waiting on me to position myself to hear His voice.

I found many instances in the Bible of times when God spoke to people, but I was particularly encouraged by 1 Samuel 3, which tells the story of a little boy who heard the voice of God. I'd heard the story of Samuel many times as a child, but when I really began to study it, the Holy Spirit illuminated it. I can't tell you what it meant to me to know that God spoke to a child who didn't immediately recognize His voice. That told me that He speaks to regular people like you and me who don't always get it right the first time either.

You see, I'm afraid we easily fall into the trap of believing that

God speaks only to some kind of spiritual elite. Most of us have the problem of comparing our insides to other people's outsides. We know about our own struggles and sins, but others, especially those we look up to in the faith, look so *good*. So we find ourselves believing that God speaks to them, but not to us. That's one of the reasons I find Samuel's story so encouraging. If the God who spun the galaxies across the heavens cared enough to talk to a young boy, I can believe Him when He says He wants to speak to me.

My examination of the first ten verses in 1 Samuel 3 revealed six things about Samuel that positioned him to hear clearly from God. In *He Speaks to Me*, I examine these six traits and explore ways we can implement them in our own lives so we will also be able to hear God and respond when He speaks.

Keep in mind that we cannot make God speak. Please don't search these pages for a magic formula to hear from Him. God is sovereign, and He resists all attempts to control or manipulate Him. He speaks to whom He chooses, when He chooses, for reasons He chooses. But that doesn't mean we're helpless. We can do two very important things.

First, because we know that God sometimes uses silence as a form of judgment, we can cooperate with the Holy Spirit to rid our life of any known sin. Second, we can remember that conversation takes two. We must yield to the promptings of the Holy Spirit as He opens our spiritual ears and become consciously aware of God working in and around us as He seeks to communicate with us. These two goals will guide our journey together in *He Speaks to Me*.

Since this book is intended to be practical, at the end of each chapter I ask you to pause for a moment and take a GPS reading. You're probably familiar with the Global Positioning System, or GPS. It's a satellite system that not only helps you determine your precise location but also helps get you where you're going. It's free, anyone can use it, and nowadays it's in cars, boats, planes, and even laptop computers. Soon it will be as universal as the telephone.

There's another GPS that's been around a lot longer than the

Global Positioning System. I call it *God's Positioning System,* and you can find it in the Bible. It's also free, already universal, and you don't need a complex system of satellites to use it. It will tell you where you are, how to get where you're going, and how much progress you've made so far. By answering a few simple questions, you'll quickly see if you are getting into a position where you can hear from God. Once you find out what's keeping you from hearing clearly from Him, you'll know what you need to do to reposition yourself.

Now let's begin to prepare ourselves to hear from God. He is calling you by name. He has a special package with your name on it, and He's waiting for you to open it. May God bless you as you seek to hear and respond to what He has for you.

Priscilla Shirer

PART ONE

A Simple Relationship

Then *the boy Samuel* ministered
to the Lord before Eli.

—1 Samuel 3:1 NKJV

❖

The first thing Scripture wants to make sure we

understand about Samuel is that he was still a child. Many

children have an openness and *willingness* that God wants

all of us to have. They are naturally curious and delight in

discovering new truths. The Lord wants us to recapture

these traits from childhood, for they point to reverence

for God, humility, and total trust.

A Childlike Simplicity

❖

I praise you, Father, Lord of heaven and earth, be-
cause you have hidden these things from the wise
and learned, and revealed them to little children.

—Matthew 11:25

❖

Not long ago I spoke at a women's conference in Maryland. There was a time of praise and worship before I got up to speak, and as soon as the music began, I noticed a young lady out of the corner of my eye.

It was hard not to notice Ryan.

At the sound of the first notes, she threw her hands straight up in the air over her head and began to clap wildly. She sang loudly—

so loudly that at one point I could actually hear her voice over the praise and worship team. And they were using mics! That teenage girl was serious about praise and worship. I mean, she was *passionate*. At one point, she even danced right out of her seat, down the aisle, and up to the front of the room.

Of course, we more mature, sedate believers were worshiping God as well—in a refined, upscale kind of way—and pretending not to notice Ryan's enthusiasm. In my peripheral vision I saw her mom reach out and grab Ryan's shirt to pull her back to her seat, but Ryan didn't care. She wanted to praise God. So her hands stayed in the air and she clapped and sang loudly as she worshiped Him with abandon.

By then I was no longer watching Ryan out of the corner of my eye. She had captured my full attention. There was just something about her that attracted me.

After the event was over, I asked about her. I learned that she is a two-year-old trapped in the body of a seventeen-year-old. You see, Ryan is autistic. She hasn't learned that her style of worship should please and impress people. Her worship hasn't been tainted with religious pomp and circumstance. She doesn't pay attention to the people around her or worry about what they might think of her. Out of her childlike relationship with her Savior, Ryan just gives Him everything she has.

We need to ask ourselves if we have a childlike relationship with the Lord. Have we become too grown-up to receive what Jesus Christ has for us? Too dignified to respond as spontaneously and wholeheartedly to Him as a child would? If so, that could be one reason we don't hear His voice more clearly.

A NOVICE WILLING TO LEARN

At first, I missed the detail that Samuel was a boy when God spoke to him. In fact, I had almost finished my study before it occurred to me that "the boy Samuel" might be the three most important words in the chapter.

The nation was full of grown-ups God could have spoken to, and the most likely one to hear from Him was right in the next room. With Eli's title and status, you'd think God would have spoken to him. He was the high priest, for heaven's sake! But God bypassed all the adults in Israel to speak to a boy. What was it about Samuel that made God choose him? First Samuel 3:7 seems to indicate that it was Samuel's childlike simplicity.

"Fearing God" means reverencing God's majesty and respecting His power.

The first part of this verse tells us that Samuel "did not yet know the LORD." At the time God spoke to him, he was not yet wise or learned. He had knowledge about God but not the wisdom that comes from knowing Him experientially. Did you know there's a difference between knowledge and wisdom? Although we often use these words interchangeably, knowledge is a natural thing, while wisdom is a spiritual thing. Someone once said that knowledge comes from looking around, while wisdom comes from looking up.

As they grow, children add to their knowledge as a matter of course. Depending on IQ and inclination, some accumulate more than others. But wisdom doesn't come naturally to us. No one becomes wise without applying spiritual insights that come only from God, and God reveals them to people who fear Him.

I know that when I speak of fearing God, I run the risk of being misunderstood. Many women who have suffered abuse tend to equate fearing God with the fear they feel in the presence of the evil, unpredictable people who have harmed them. Please remember that God is anything but unpredictable.

God is love . . . all the time.

God is good . . . all the time.

Fearing God doesn't mean that we should feel the way an abused child does in the presence of a raging parent. In the Bible, "fearing

God" means reverencing God's majesty and respecting His power.

"The fear of the Lord" is essential to hearing from God because it prepares us for what God has to say and enables us to apply what He tells us to our lives. It is so important that Solomon repeats the phrase eleven times in Proverbs.

Proverbs 1:7 says, "The fear of the LORD is the beginning of knowledge." The word "knowledge" here actually means *spiritual understanding*, and the word "beginning" means *prerequisite*, so the sentence can read like this: "Reverence for the LORD is the prerequisite for spiritual understanding." And Proverbs 9:10 says, "The fear of the LORD is the beginning of *wisdom*."

Notice the progression: Proverbs 1:7 promises that respecting God will lead to spiritual understanding, while Proverbs 9:10 promises that it will also lead to wisdom. Fearing God not only opens the door to spiritual insights, it also goes a step further and allows us to skillfully apply those insights so that they can transform our lives in practical ways.

I don't know about you, but *proven skill* matters much more to me than knowledge. What good is knowledge if we don't know how to apply it wisely? If I were going to parachute out of an airplane, I'd much rather go skydiving with someone who had jumped and landed successfully dozens of times rather than with someone who had just read dozens of books on the subject.

Intellectual knowledge can help us know about God, but only a personal relationship with Him will lead us to saving knowledge, because that's what leads us to respect God. In fact, Isaiah 33:6 says that the fear of the Lord is the key to the rich store not only of salvation but also of wisdom and knowledge. We cannot expect to hear God's voice if we begin at the wrong place. Reverencing God opens our spiritual ears to hear clearly from Him.

Although Samuel "did not yet know the LORD," he had begun at the right place. He had positioned himself to acquire knowledge and wisdom, and his spiritual ears were open to hear God's voice. Because he reverenced God, he was also prepared to obey God's word when it came.

A CHILD WILLING TO OBEY

When Samuel first heard God's voice, he thought Eli was calling him, and he responded immediately. The boy's obedience flowed out of his relationship with his mentor. Because he respected him, he obeyed him.

To hear God's voice, we also must be willing to respond appropriately to Him. Ecclesiastes 12:12 says, "Of making many books there is no end, and much study wearies the body." Though we sometimes think we can please God by plowing through a stack of books on theology, we can get so wrapped up in accumulating knowledge about religion that we forget the simple truth tucked away in the next verse: "The last and final word is this: Fear God. Do what he tells you" (THE MESSAGE).

I was a rebellious teenager. I hate to admit it, but it is true. Whenever my parents told me I couldn't do something, I immediately found a way to do it. The "no dating rule" translated to "go out with the group, but just couple off once you get there." The "no talking to boys on the phone rule" translated to "wait until everyone goes to sleep for the night, and then call them." When I wasn't allowed to wear makeup, I would just put it on after I got to school. More often than not, I would get caught.

I clearly remember my parents saying, "You don't respect us, because if you did you would obey us. If you would obey us, we would have a better relationship." At the time I didn't see any correlation between respect, obedience, and relationship, but time has proved that, once again, my parents knew what they were talking about. (Don't you hate it when your parents are right?) When you and I respect someone, our actions automatically reflect it.

Our ability to hear God's voice begins when we reverence Him through simple obedience. That is the basis of the childlike relationship He desires with you and me. Knowing God is not enough; we must fear and obey Him.

AN AMATEUR RECEPTIVE TO REVELATION

After telling us that Samuel "did not yet know the LORD," 1 Samuel 3:7 goes on to say that "the word of the LORD had not yet been revealed" to him. The boy did not regularly receive direct revelations from God. He wasn't a pro at this. In fact, he was an amateur. He had no experience at all in hearing directly from God. That's why at first he didn't know what was going on. But that didn't stop God from speaking to him, and it didn't keep Samuel from listening.

Be encouraged if the idea of hearing God's voice is new for you. It was new for Samuel too. Remember that God had to call Samuel three times. If you don't get it the first time, God will call again.

As near as we can tell, Samuel was around twelve when God spoke to him. Eli had been his mentor for nine years by then, so the boy probably knew that God usually spoke through prophets. However, Samuel was open to the unusual way in which God chose to speak to him. Young people are teachable because they are still receptive to new experiences.

Samuel was willing to accept what God had to say and how He chose to say it.

I wonder how many of us would have accepted God's unconventional method. When God wants to do something out of the ordinary, can He look to you or me? Or will He have to bypass us because we've become too set in our ways? Does He just know we'd say, "But we never did it that way before"? Sometimes we try to put God in our little denominational, traditional, or comfortable boxes and assume He operates only within those boundaries. So when He wants to do something outside those boundaries, He can't do it with us.

Samuel didn't spend a lot of time second-guessing God's message. He didn't pick it apart, challenge it, or criticize it. He just listened to it and accepted it. Sometimes it's just better not to know so much. Did you know that, aerodynamically speaking, it's impossible for bumblebees to fly? Science books say that the body of a bumblebee is too heavy for the weight of its wings. But because bumblebees don't know any better, they just fly.

God chose to break years of silence in an unconventional way, and Samuel was willing to accept what God had to say and how He chose to say it. People who have a childlike relationship with God listen to Him and accept His revelation however it comes.

When I met Ryan at that conference in Maryland, I wondered if I might be missing out on what she was experiencing because she just didn't know any better. In the midst of a throng of presumably more mature, educated, experienced believers, this one girl was expressing her childlike relationship with the Lord with passion and enthusiasm because that was all she knew. *Who is really better off?* I asked myself.

Do you want to hear God's voice? Then you must become like a child, for when the Lord said that "the kingdom of heaven belongs to such as these" (Matthew 19:14), He was talking about people like Samuel and Ryan—people who have a simple, childlike relationship with Him.

WHERE ARE YOU NOW?

❖

TAKE TIME FOR A GPS READING:

- The last time I heard from God through Scripture, what was my reaction?

- How do I expect God to speak to me?

- What evidence do I have that the knowledge I've attained in life has made me more like Christ?

- How would I react if someone like Ryan were to sit next to me in church?

❖ ❖ ❖

Father, I thank You for the great privilege of being Your child. I reverence Your majesty and power. Lord, as I think about what it means to have a simple relationship with You, remind me of the childlike characteristics You want to see in me. Help me put aside my traditions and religious prejudices so that I will be completely willing to receive both Your message and the way You want to give it to me. Then help me respond to You like a child—obediently, spontaneously, and wholeheartedly.

❖ ❖ ❖

A Humble Approach

❖

Whoever humbles himself like this child is the

greatest in the kingdom of heaven.

—Matthew 18:4

❖

When I was one year old, my parents helped found Oak Cliff Bible Fellowship Church. As a preacher's kid, I got used to everyone catering to me and making a big deal out of everything I did. The sad result was that I wasn't very humble. When I was about eighteen, it finally dawned on me that I was in trouble, and I made a conscious decision to learn to humble myself.

Fortunately, I had a wonderful example to follow. My Aunt

Elizabeth is one of the humblest people I know. She has faithfully served in our church for more than twenty-five years. Her car is often the first one in the parking lot and the last to leave after service on Sunday mornings.

She goes about her work quietly and unobtrusively. Her outstanding characteristic is meekness. She never puts herself forward, tries to make a name for herself, or claims credit for what she does. She rarely receives public recognition for the wonderful job she does with the children at our church, but that doesn't matter. She doesn't do what she does so people will praise her. She does it to please God. Like the children she works with, Aunt Elizabeth has humility.

A SURPRISING EXAMPLE

The disciples lived with Jesus. For three years they heard Him preach and watched Him heal the sick. They saw Him feed five thousand people with only five barley loaves and two fish. They even saw Him walk on water. Yet when Jesus wanted to teach His disciples about humility, He didn't dazzle them with miracles. He pointed to a little child. Can you imagine how the disciples must have felt when Jesus called a little child to their midst and said, "I tell you the truth, unless you change and become like little children, you will never enter the kingdom of heaven" (Matthew 18:3). What a blow to the disciples' egos—not to mention their plans!

The disciples came to Jesus and asked, "Who is the greatest in the kingdom of heaven?" (Matthew 18:1). Notice that they weren't asking *what kind of people* would be greatest in the kingdom of heaven. They wanted to know which one of *them* would be greatest, and they were arguing about it—again. Not much has changed in two thousand years. Today, we seek to be the best Brownie mom, have the best house, drive the best car, have the best job, dress our children in the best clothes while attending the best schools. Pride even spills over into our churches as ministries seek top positioning during the week's announcements. Any way possible, we seek to have our name in lights.

The disciples' self-focused ways of thinking wouldn't be resolved that day. Angling for top spots in the kingdom, James and John got their mom in on the act, and she later approached Jesus to speak on their behalf. When Jesus asked Mrs. Zebedee what she wanted Him to do for her, she said, "Grant that one of these two sons of mine may sit at your right and the other at your left in your kingdom" (Matthew 20:21). Jesus gently explained that His Father already had people in mind for those positions. When the other disciples heard about the request, they became angry with the two brothers. They quickly became divided when each became obsessed with his own greatness.

From the start of their roles as disciples, Jesus told them He had plans for them. To the fishermen sons of Zebedee He'd said, "Come, follow me, and I will make you fishers of men" (4:19). They had left behind their vocations for a special calling. Now, in order to fulfill that calling, Jesus was asking them to leave behind their plans for greatness and strive for childlike humility.

The Peril of Pride

Pride ruins relationships in homes, jobs, schools, and churches. It causes husbands to abuse their authority, wives to refuse to submit, and children to rebel against their parents. Under the influence of pride, an employer ignores the needs of her staff, students refuse the sound instructions of the teacher, and a friend refuses to ask for forgiveness. Time and time again I have experienced friction in my relationships with my friends or family members, and when I truly search to see what the root problem is, I come face-to-face with my persistent pride. Think about this one for a moment. Do you currently have any strained relationships? If so, ask the Lord to check the condition of your heart. Ask Him to reveal to you where pride is getting in the way of reconciliation.

One of Jesus' less frequently mentioned parables has long been one of my favorites. He said that when you're invited to a banquet, you shouldn't take a seat at the head table, for if a more distinguished guest arrives, you're going to be very embarrassed when the host asks you to move. But if you sit at the foot of the table, your host just might honor you by asking you to move to a better seat (Luke 14:7–11). Far too frequently, I find that I have seated myself in the wrong place.

On another occasion Jesus spoke to "some who had great self-confidence and scorned everyone else" (Luke 18:9 NLT). The disciples were a part of that group. No doubt the Messiah had made sure of that. The story He told was about a Pharisee and a tax collector who both go up to the temple to pray.

In Jesus' day, Pharisees set the standard for righteousness among the Jews. They considered themselves authorities on God's law, and scrupulously observed ceremonial washings, fasting, and almsgiving. Tax collectors, on the other hand, were shunned as the worst kind of sinners. They were hired by the Romans and often extorted money from their own people. The Pharisees hated tax collectors because they were dishonest and considered them traitors because they worked for Rome.

Believers could accomplish much greater things for the kingdom of God if they didn't care who got the credit for it.

When the Pharisee went to the temple to pray, he stood up, took center stage, and prayed aloud—about himself. He thanked God that he was a holy and just man who tithed and fasted and wasn't a robber, evildoer, adulterer, or—heaven forbid!—a tax collector like that man over there in the corner. The tax collector, however, knew he was a sinner. He was standing at a distance, afraid to even lift his eyes to heaven. Instead, he was beating his breast and imploring God to have mercy on him (vv. 11–13).

Jesus ended the parable by saying that the tax collector, not the Pharisee, went home righteous before God. Then, not wanting to leave the disciples in any doubt about the meaning of the parable,

He made the application for them: "Everyone who exalts himself will be humbled, and he who humbles himself will be exalted" (v. 14).

People who humble themselves do not think more of themselves than they ought or try to show others how great they are. Like my Aunt Elizabeth, truly humble people use the gifts God has given them without bragging about them as if they are the result of their own doing.

Pride is not only the compost heap on which myriad other problems and sins grow, but it also guarantees God's opposition. Both James 4:6 and 1 Peter 5:5 say that "God opposes the proud." Let that sink in for a moment. When we allow pride in our lives, we whistle for God's opposition. Pride is *first* on the list of things that God hates most (see Proverbs 6:17). It's the sin that got Lucifer thrown out of heaven, and it can keep people out of heaven too if they refuse the Savior.

Immediately after Jesus finished telling the parable of the Pharisee and the tax collector, as if on cue, some little children were brought to Him. The disciples rebuked the children, but Jesus called the children to Him and instructed His disciples to let them come, saying, "Anyone who will not receive the kingdom of God like a little child will never enter it" (Luke 18:17).

I once heard someone say that believers could accomplish much greater things for the kingdom of God if they didn't care who got the credit for it. Pride, the antithesis of humility, makes us think that we deserve special treatment, recognition, or honor. It causes us to think too little of others and too much of ourselves. Pride leads us to force our way into a situation, while humility waits.

The Product of Pride

Pride always produces faulty expectations. I can detect pride in my life when I start to expect things to turn out "my way" and am disappointed when they do not. Pride causes us to make assumptions that set us up to miss out on what God wants for us and the way He wants to accomplish it.

For example, the Jews were intensely interested in the kingdom of heaven. They had their own ideas about what it would look like and how it would come. The expression "kingdom of God" or "kingdom of heaven" originated with the Old Testament Jews, who looked with great expectation for God's direct, divine intervention in their history. They wanted to see His fingerprints on their lives and His handiwork in their nation. So they looked forward to the coming of the Messiah and labeled His arrival and intervention in their historical circumstances the "kingdom of heaven."

God's plan was so completely different
from what the disciples expected that
it didn't make any sense to them,
and they couldn't accept it.

In Jesus' day, the Jews were certain that the Messiah was coming any day to free them from their oppressors and restore Israel. They understood this to mean that He would use His power to throw out the Roman government and set up His own kingdom there. Unlike the Pharisees, who didn't believe that Jesus was the Messiah, Jesus' disciples *knew* the Messiah had come (Matthew 16:16). However, they too believed that the kingdom of heaven would come when the Messiah set up His kingdom in Israel. The change they were looking for was *external*.

The only problem with this scenario was that the kingdom Jesus had come to establish was centered on the state of their souls, not on the state of their nation. The change He was looking for was *internal*. Moreover, He had just told them that He was about to be crucified, not crowned.

God's plan was so completely different from what the disciples expected that it didn't make any sense to them, and they couldn't accept it. They were so sure they knew how and when the kingdom would come (and so concerned about their own place in it) that they weren't really listening to what Jesus said.

Often Jesus wants to reveal important information to us, but our pride causes us to have preconceived notions that get in the way of our ability to hear what He is saying.

Jesus used children to teach humility to the disciples because children have few such preconceived ideas. We adults are often sure we know exactly what God will do and how He will do it. We are often closed to new possibilities; children are open to them. We often aren't willing to come to God on His terms; children are. Sometimes unknowingly, we place impossible expectations on our friends, spouses, children, marriages, and even on ourselves that are not in line with God's desires for us. When these expectations are not met, we become disgruntled with our lives and with our God. Humility, on the other hand, clears the pathway for us to hear God because it keeps us open to the way God wants to speak and move in our lives.

The Cure for Pride

Jesus had already told His disciples not only that His kingdom was not of this earth, but also that it was already among them. His plan to restore communion between God and man and create the opportunity for divine intimacy was already under way, but they didn't see it. "The kingdom of God is near. Repent and believe the good news!" He had said (Mark 1:15). The message to the Jews was "open your eyes!" What you've been looking for is right here and right now, standing right in front of you in the person of Jesus. To receive the kingdom, all you have to do is humble yourself like a child and admit that you don't have it all together and that you need a Savior.

That's the same message God has for us today. Friend, Jesus is watching you as you read the pages of this book that today you will "open your eyes" and see all that He has to offer you. He's saying, "The kingdom of God—His direct divine intervention in your life— can belong to you." Become like a child, and it will be yours. Simply surrender to the Holy Spirit's humbling work in you.

Over and over in Scripture, God assures us that childlike humility is key to positioning ourselves to hear from Him. "'I live in a high and holy place,'" God says, "'but also with him who is contrite and lowly in spirit'" (Isaiah 57:15). "'This is the one I esteem: he who is humble and contrite in spirit, and trembles at my word'" (Isaiah 66:2).

Jesus is the best example we have of true humility. He is the visible manifestation of the God of the universe, who "stoops down"— humbles Himself—to behold all His creatures, though He is infinitely above them (Psalm 113:6). Philippians 2:8 says that Jesus loves us so much that "he humbled himself and became obedient to death— even death on a cross!"

As the ministry the Lord has given my family grows, I am often asked if it is more difficult to be humble. My answer is that it could be if my heart's passion weren't to get to know God and hear His voice. The more time I spend with Him in His Word and the more He reveals Himself to me, the more I realize how gracious He has been to me and how much I need Him. I know that apart from Him I could do nothing. Humility keeps the lines of communication open between God and me.

Knowing all that the Lord has done for us, given us, and forgiven us, humility should be the natural outpouring of our thankful hearts. When we approach God humbly and bow down before Him, we put ourselves in a position to hear from Him.

WHERE ARE YOU NOW?

TAKE TIME FOR A GPS READING:

- To what do I usually attribute my achievements and successes in life?

- What are some preconceived expectations I have in the different areas of my life that might keep me from hearing from God?

- Who are the people with whom I have a strained relationship? How does pride play a part in this?

- How can I know that I am experiencing God's promise of the kingdom of heaven in my life right now?

❖ ❖ ❖

*Father, I confess that pride often separates me from You
and others, that my preconceived notions often keep me
from knowing the truth, and that my plans are often not
Your plans. Thank You for reminding me how important
childlike humility is to You and how much You hate pride.
Thank You, Lord, for humbling Yourself and dying on the
cross so that I could live forever with You in Your kingdom.
As I bow in humility before You in my actions and atti-
tudes, I look forward to hearing You speak clearly to me.*

❖ ❖ ❖

A Simple Trust

❖

Don't worry about having enough food or drink or
clothing. Why be like the pagans who are so deeply
concerned about these things? Your heavenly
Father already knows all your needs.

—Matthew 6:31–32 NLT

❖

When I was a child, every August we took a month-long vacation. We would all pile into the van and drive somewhere across the country. One year we drove to Arizona to see the Grand Canyon. I remember that trip specifically because when we got to Flagstaff, we couldn't find a hotel with a vacancy. We were all tired and ready to go to bed, but there was no place for us to sleep.

After we had tried a lot of hotels, my little brother said, "Dad, we didn't pray about it."

"Oh yeah," my dad said. "Well, I guess we should pray about it."

So we prayed, and within minutes a hotel attendant tracked us down to tell us that a room had miraculously opened up. It took a child to remember to trust God for everything.

CHILDLIKE TRUST

By now we know for sure that Jesus welcomes children. The Greek word Luke used for children means an "infant" (Luke 18:17). You need to know that because there's a difference between an infant and a toddler. Let me tell you how I know: I've had both—at once. Our older son, Jackson, was just getting into the toddler stage when his little brother, Jerry Jr., came along. Trust me, there's a difference between toddlers and infants.

When Jackson was approaching the terrible twos, he started to think he just didn't need me anymore. He didn't want me to help him with anything. He had an opinion about what food he wanted to eat, what he wanted to drink, and what clothes he wanted to put on. And he was starting to think he could do it all himself. When I tried to help him, he would say, "No, Mommy, no!"

Jerry Jr. was still just a baby then, and he depended on me for everything. If I didn't feed him, he didn't eat. If I didn't change his diaper, he stayed dirty. He knew he needed help, and he expected me to come through for him. That's how God wants us to depend on Him—as completely as infants depend on their mother.

As we become more physically mature, the more self-sufficient we become. But spiritual maturity should have the opposite effect. The more spiritually mature we become, the more we should rely on God. Christ wants us to have a childlike trust in Him. The Greek word used to refer to this kind of faith is *pisteuo*, which means "to place complete confidence in." Childlike people trust God for everything.

THE TRUST GAME

My sister and I used to play a "trust game." Chrystal would stand behind me, and I would close my eyes and fall back into her arms. On one occasion she allowed me to fall back into her arms five or six times without incident. Every time she caught me, she built up my confidence in her. However, on the seventh time, she really let me down—literally. She stepped away, and I went crashing to the floor. The betrayal of trust hurt much worse than the landing.

As we become adults, trusting often becomes difficult for us. We not only become more self-sufficient, but hurtful life experiences also undermine our ability to trust. I've known women who have suffered the most extreme betrayals. Some were beaten, burned with cigarettes, or locked in closets by the very people who should have been protecting them. As a result, they can't really trust anyone. Perhaps you haven't experienced anything that extreme. Maybe a boyfriend broke your heart or a friend told your secret. But the bottom line is that sooner or later we all experience the betrayal of our trust.

How do we know we trust God?
By doing what He says.

Yet Jesus still wants us to approach Him with total trust. No matter how often people betray us, we all have to practice trusting Christ. For, you see, faith is a growing thing. None of us are standing still in our faith. We're either learning to trust God more . . . or we're drifting away from Him.

Rest assured that God is worthy of complete trust. I tried to make a list of people I can place great confidence in, but it was pretty short. Only one has earned my *complete* confidence. The Lord will never betray us. At the moment of salvation, He asks us to trust Him, but He doesn't stop there. God continually asks us to keep falling back into His waiting arms.

THE REWARDS OF TRUST

The writer of Hebrews tells us that "without faith it is impossible to please God, because anyone who comes to him must believe that he exists and that he rewards those who earnestly seek him" (11:6). This passage assures us that God rewards the confidence we place in Him. How do we know we trust God? By doing what He says. We see this truth portrayed vividly in the experiences of the children of Israel.

Although the Israelites wandered in the wilderness for forty years as a result of their rebellion against God, they survived because God rewarded them when they did what He told them to do.

As soon as the Israelites found themselves in the desert, the old slavery of Egypt started to look pretty good to them, and they began to grumble against Moses. "If only we had died by the LORD's hand in Egypt!" they cried. "There we sat around pots of meat and ate all the food we wanted, but you have brought us out into this desert to starve this entire assembly to death" (Exodus 16:3).

The Lord told Moses that He would provide food for the Israelites by raining down daily bread from heaven (v. 4). All the people had to do was gather as much as they needed. If they tried to disobey and gather more than they needed, they had to eat maggots, so they quickly learned to follow God's instructions. For forty years the Hebrews survived in the wilderness because God sent them manna to eat. God was teaching them that He rewards those who demonstrate their trust in Him by doing what He says.

God knows what His children need
and often pours out His grace
despite our unbelief.

Food wasn't the only thing in short supply in the desert . . . so was water, and several times the Israelites thought they were going to die of thirst. When the Israelites reached Rephidim, there was no water, and they again blamed Moses: "Why did you bring us up out of Egypt to make us and our children and livestock die of thirst?" (Exodus 17:3).

This time, Moses was the one whose faith was rewarded. God told Moses to take his staff—the same one that had brought the plagues down on Egypt and parted the Red Sea—and strike the rock at Horeb. Moses followed God's instructions, and life-giving water gushed out of the rock. The way the Israelites asked for water revealed their lack of trust in Him, but God gave them water anyway because He knew they needed it. God knows what His children need and often pours out His grace despite our unbelief.

THE CONSEQUENCES OF UNBELIEF

Just as trust leads to rewards, lack of it can lead to loss. Thirty-eight years after the water shortage at Rephidim, Moses gave us an example of how failure to do what God says can lead to loss of reward.

When the Israelites reached Kadesh, once again there was no water. And once again they accused Moses. "Why did you bring us up out of Egypt to this terrible place?" they asked. After grumbling about their diet again, they exclaimed, "And there is no water to drink!" (Numbers 20:5).

Once again, God planned to provide water from the rock to satisfy His people (v. 11). This time, He told Moses and Aaron to take the staff and call the people to assemble. Then Moses was to speak to the rock in front of the Israelites, and it would pour out water for them. Moses gathered the community in front of the rock as God told him to, but instead of speaking to the rock, he struck it with the staff.

The people received the water they needed, but both Moses and Aaron paid a heavy price. God said, "'Because you did not trust in me enough to honor me as holy in the sight of the Israelites, you will not bring this community into the land I give them'" (v. 12). Moses had prayed that he would see the Promised Land, but God did not honor his request because Moses failed to honor Him.

Notice that God's punishment was not just for disobeying. Look carefully at verse 12 again. God says, *"Because you did not trust in me."* Failure to do exactly what God asks, regardless of how strange or incomplete His instructions may seem, shows that we don't trust Him. It shows we don't believe that He is God and knows what's best. When we don't do what God tells us to do, we are saying that we don't think He is wise enough or capable enough to handle our situations.

I admit that sometimes when God's instructions seem strange, I rebel against them. God's way is always better, but sometimes I still fail to trust Him. For example, there are times when I want to say something specific to my husband, even though I know that the Lord is clearly instructing me to keep my mouth shut. In such instances, every time I speak, I wish I hadn't. My words only escalate arguments and cause discord in our relationship. I may win an argument by not trusting what I hear from God, but there's always a price to pay.

A GOD WHO COMES THROUGH

It was July 23, 2004—a week too soon, according to the expected due date of our second child. However, it seemed that this baby didn't care what I'd been told, for the pains that accompany childbirth came upon me early that day. The cramping continued, but I didn't want to go to the hospital until I was sure this was the real thing. When my discomfort no longer left any room for doubt, Jerry rushed me to the hospital. The doctor checked my progress and reported that I was nine centimeters dilated and almost ready to push.

However, there was a problem: the baby's head was still very high in my body. My mind flashed back to Jackson's birth. The same thing had happened then. His head hadn't descended into the birth canal either, and after I had pushed unsuccessfully for three hours, he had to be delivered by C-section. Now I prepared myself for the inevitable —another C-section.

The doctor tried everything imaginable to get my baby's head down, but nothing worked. Finally he suggested that I just try pushing to see if I could push his head down where it needed to be. I pushed as hard as I could, and as I did, I saw the doctor's eyes light up and heard my mother and sister squeal in delight. The baby's head miraculously descended and began to crown!

The doctor quickly put on his scrubs and called for his nurse. He looked at me and said, "I've never seen anything like this before. We're going to have a baby here!" Ten minutes later, Jerry Jr. was born.

As I lay in my hospital room the next day looking down at my beautiful son, I began thinking about the entries I'd made in my prayer journal during my pregnancy. For many months I had prayed that this one would end differently than the first. I had asked the Lord to help me go into labor at home and complete most of it there so I could avoid a long hospital stay. I had asked Him to allow the baby to come a little earlier than expected so he might be a little smaller than my first son and maybe fit through the birth canal. And I had prayed that a C-section wouldn't be necessary this time around.

God answered every one of my prayers, yet when He did, we were all shocked that it had happened just the way I had prayed. Why were we so surprised? I think perhaps it was because we didn't really think He could or would come through for us.

Trusting the Lord implies that we expect Him to come through for us. Sometimes I think the more mature we get, the less we expect that the Lord will answer our prayers. That could be one reason we don't pray about everything.

Jesus declared, "If you believe, you will receive whatever you ask for in prayer" (Matthew 21:22). Do the Savior's words mean that we can order up whatever we want in prayer and receive it through faith? I think not. I think the example of Moses shows us that obedient faith can make the difference between answered prayer and corrective discipline.

We don't need to place our faith in our faith, as if our belief controlled the power of God. What we do need to do is believe and obey God, thus placing ourselves in a position for God to bless us fully.

Could the cause of our unanswered prayers be our lack of childlike trust? I think the answer in Scripture is very clear.

You are reading a book about hearing the voice of God. Do you really believe that God will speak to you? If you find yourself doubting, God has a message for you: You're not going to be hearing from Him anytime soon. James says that those who doubt shouldn't think they will receive anything from the Lord (1:6–7).

The boy Samuel had the kind of simple trust that the Lord wants us to have. Samuel heard someone call his name three times, and each time he was sure it was Eli. The priest himself was slow to understand what was happening, but when he got it, he told Samuel, "Go and lie down, and if he calls you, say, 'Speak, LORD, for your servant is listening'" (1 Samuel 3:9).

Notice that Samuel's response wasn't "you've got to be kidding me." He had complete confidence that what Eli had told him was the truth, and he did what the priest told him to do. As a result of simple trust, Samuel heard God's voice.

WHERE ARE YOU NOW?

❖

TAKE TIME FOR A GPS READING:

- How has my faith in the Lord grown since I first entered into a relationship with Him?

- What are some of the small things I depend on the Lord for?

- How does my life confirm that God rewards those who trust Him?

- How do I think God feels when I don't really expect Him to come through for me?

❖ ❖ ❖

Lord, I confess that I often do not fully trust You. Show me those areas where I operate outside the realm of faith. Show me when I'm not obeying Your instructions because I think my way is better. Help me do exactly what You want me to do. Forgive me for the times I don't pray about everything because I'm not really sure You'll come through for me. Remove any doubt I have that You will speak to me, for I want to hear from You as Samuel did.

❖ ❖ ❖

PART TWO

A Single-Minded Worship

The boy Samuel *ministered to the Lord* before Eli.

—1 Samuel 3:1 NKJV

❖

The second thing we discover about Samuel is that

he was a *worshiper.* In fact, the phrase "Samuel was

ministering to the LORD" appears at least three times before

we get to 1 Samuel 3. This means that worshiping God was

a part of Samuel's routine and character. He knew what

worship was all about, and he didn't let anyone or anything

distract him from doing what mattered most—giving

God all the glory He deserves.

*Glory
to God*

❖

Ascribe to the LORD glory and strength.

Ascribe to the LORD the glory due his name;

worship the LORD in the splendor of his holiness.

—Psalm 29:1–2

❖

First Samuel 3:1 (NKJV) says, "The boy Samuel ministered to the Lord *before Eli.*" When the boy was three years old, his mother had dropped him off at the temple for Eli to raise. By the time God chose to reveal Himself to Samuel, Eli had spent about nine years teaching Samuel everything he needed to know about temple duties and what it meant to minister to the Lord.

"Ministering to the Lord before Eli" means that Samuel's mentor was standing right there while he worshiped. Now, I don't know about you, but if my mentor was standing right beside me, I would want to impress her. I would want to make sure she knew that I had this worship thing down. I would be worshiping God, yes, but out of the corner of my eye I would be watching to see if Eli knew I was doing a good job.

But the text is clear. It says that Samuel was ministering to the Lord even though he was standing in the presence of Eli. Samuel didn't allow Eli to distract him. He was single-minded about giving God the glory due His name because he knew what worship was all about—single-minded, undistracted devotion.

WHAT'S IT ALL ABOUT?

A few years ago I spoke at what was for me an unusual venue. Normally I speak to very large audiences—two thousand women or more—so I was excited to be able to minister to fifty women from a small church in Florida.

Most conferences are wonderfully organized. The sponsors fly in professional singers, decorate the stage, and check the microphones to make sure that the sound system is in perfect working order. This conference was none of the above. The decor wasn't anything to write home about, the microphones hadn't been balanced, and the only credential needed to sing in the praise and worship team was to be able to make a joyful noise. That was it.

The circumstances were so unusual for me that I knew God had brought me there to teach me something, and I asked Him a very direct question: *Lord, what is it You have for me here?* I know that the Lord has a reason for everything, and I wanted to know very specifically why He had chosen to place me there.

Those women loved God, and the event started out great. But as it went on, I felt I was missing something. Nothing was registering with me, and I felt I wasn't hearing from God. So I kept praying, *Lord, what do You have for me?*

Then as the emcee was making her closing remarks, a woman sitting in the corner began to rock back and forth and cry rivers of tears.

She didn't say anything out loud or call attention to herself, but we could hear her moaning and crying. After a few minutes, the emcee stopped and said, "You know what? Let's just pray with our sister. Whatever she's going through, let's just stop the program and pray with her."

I wish I'd had a video camera with me so I could show you what happened next. For the next couple of hours those women worshiped God. Some stood, some got on their knees, and some lay prostrate on the floor, but all of them worshiped God. No one seemed concerned that the program had taken a detour. No one seemed concerned about pleasing or impressing other women in the room. I didn't see anyone looking at her watch or slipping quietly out the back door because she had something better to do. These women were single-mindedly worshiping God.

Someone started a song, and everybody joined in.

"Just ask, says the Lord God of hosts, and I will answer you," someone called from the back of the room.

"Lord, I want to hear Your voice. When I leave this place, I never want to be the same again," someone else called out.

Nobody said, "Lord, give me a brand-new car," or "Lord, I want to make more money," or "Lord, would You give me that house on the hill?" Because they were focused on God, the result was that God showed up. And when God shows up, He takes center stage. The only thing that mattered that day was that God was there and everybody was worshiping Him.

God chooses to speak to those who focus on His glory.

I have never felt the presence of God as thick in a place as I did that day. It was so strong that it pressed me to my knees. There I was on the floor, unable to move. I felt so unworthy that the Lord had brought me there to minister to those women. They were teaching the teacher what single-minded worship was all about.

I can remember only a handful of times when the Holy Spirit has spoken so clearly to me. This was one of those times. It was as if He was sitting right there on the floor next to me. He said, *Priscilla, this is what I had for you. This is why I wanted you here. I wanted you to see that I would rather be with fifty women who are serious about worshiping Me than with five thousand who are more concerned about staging a religious event.*

Single-minded worship begins when we concentrate on God's glory. Giving God glory means giving Him the honor He deserves. When we do this, we take our eyes off ourselves and turn them on Him. God chooses to speak to those who focus on His glory.

To God Be the Glory

The book of Exodus tells us that Moses spent forty years tending sheep in the wilderness. Can you imagine how mind-numbing that must have been after spending the first forty years of his life as a prince in Pharaoh's court? But one day when Moses was the ripe old age of eighty, his life became anything but boring. That was the day God spoke to him from a burning bush. Exodus 3, which describes Moses' encounter with God, teaches us four specific lessons about God's glory. When we understand God's glory, we too want to offer Him the same kind of single-minded worship Samuel did. When we do, we are better positioned to hear His voice.

LESSON #1: *God's Glory Often Appears in Desert Places*

Moses encountered the glory of God not in a lavish palace but in a barren desert. Often we can see God's glory best in the midst of life's dry seasons. Have you walked through a dry season lately? Perhaps you're experiencing one now. Maybe you've prayed and prayed for your daughter, but she's drinking and doing drugs. Maybe you've been a devoted wife for forty years, but your husband has just left you for a younger woman. Maybe you were next in line for a promotion at work, but a less qualified friend of the boss got the job.

If you are currently in a wilderness season, be encouraged. You are in a good position to hear from God. Moses was way overqualified for the position of shepherd. Though he was raised in Pharaoh's royal household, for forty years this prince chased sheep. But Moses accepted the situation and served where he was, and God's glory eventually showed up. My sister, be faithful even in the desert seasons, and you will see that bushes will burn.

LESSON #2: *God's Glory Is Beyond Our Comprehension*

When God called to Moses from the burning bush, Moses immediately noticed that it wasn't burning up, and he couldn't understand how that could be. God's glory is always beyond human comprehension. An attempt to understand Him by restricting Him to the laws of nature or comparing Him to man minimizes His greatness and power. That's why God specifically commands us not to make idols (Deuteronomy 5:8). Worshiping idols exchanges the truth for a lie and attempts to take God's glory and give it to products of our own imaginations.

Clearly, God responds unfavorably to our attempt to humanize Him. Anytime we seek to lower God to some level we can understand, we dishonor Him and corrupt ourselves. God's glory cannot be confined. We can only point to it in the visible signs He gives us, acknowledge them, and worship Him in response.

LESSON #3: *God's Glory Is Reserved for Only One*

Fire in a dry country like Horeb would normally spread quickly, but when God met Moses there, only one bush was burning. This reminds me that God does not share His glory. Even as Christians, we often desire glory in the eyes of man. We perform and seek attention. We spend time reading our own press releases and trying to control what others think of us. We want the fire reserved for God to spread to us.

For those of you who minister in your home, neighborhood, or church, here's the best definition of ministry I've ever heard. John the Baptist was standing with two disciples when Jesus walked by. John said, "Look, the Lamb of God!" Immediately, those disciples left John to follow Jesus (John 1:29–37 NASB). Ministry is when the people who hear you don't want more of you; they want more of Him because of what you've said. When you point them to God's fire instead of trying to get attention for yourself—that's ministry.

> *Often our thoughts run to*
> *"what do they think of me?"*
> *when what we should be concerned*
> *with is "what do they think of Him?"*

Jesus warns us to beware of doing acts of righteousness so that people will admire us (Matthew 6:1). If you like people's applause, you'd better milk it for all it's worth, because it's all you're going to get. God doesn't reward our attempts to steal applause that rightfully belongs to Him.

Although God has a glory that He shares with us through Christ (2 Thessalonians 2:14), when we trespass on glory that is His alone, it is to our own peril. Often our thoughts run to "what do they think of me?" when what we should be concerned with is "what do they think of Him?" Keeping one eye on an "Eli" when you worship will keep you from focusing on the Lord and giving Him the glory He deserves. But focusing single-mindedly on gaining God's approval will pave the way for you to hear His voice.

LESSON #4: *God's Glory Demands a Response*

When God spoke from the burning bush, He told Moses to do two things: remove his shoes and come no closer. Just as He did with Moses, God gives us instructions on how to respond to His glory. In Exodus 3 we learn that when we are in God's presence, we must quickly and reverently do three things.

First, we must turn aside to look. When God's glory showed up, Moses interrupted his normal duties to respond. He turned aside (v. 3). The revealed glory of God demands that we pause, listen, and heed His voice. God waited until He saw that Moses was enamored with His glory before He gave Moses instructions for the next phase of his life. I shudder to think of the times I may have missed the clear direction of God because I refused to turn aside and look.

Second, we must confess our own unworthiness. Isaiah had one of the most famous encounters with God in history. When God appeared to him, the prophet cried out, "'Woe to me! . . . I am ruined! For I am a man of unclean lips'" (Isaiah 6:5). God told Moses to remove his sandals because he was standing on holy ground. In Moses' day, removing shoes was a token of respect. When Moses removed his sandals, he acknowledged that he was unworthy to be in God's holy presence.

Third, we must remember to fear God. Exodus 3:6 tells us that "Moses hid his face, because he was afraid to look at God." The fear he experienced was the kind of fear we talked about in chapter 1— reverence for God's majesty and respect for His power. But don't think for a moment that Moses' knees weren't knocking. Moses knew that if he tried to stand in God's presence apart from His grace, God's holiness would destroy him.

After seeing the Lord's glory, Moses set an example for us to follow: He turned aside to look, confessed his unworthiness, and feared God. These three actions will get our eyes off ourselves and others, focus them on God, and prepare our hearts to receive what He has to say to us.

WHERE ARE YOU NOW?

❖

TAKE TIME FOR A GPS READING:

- Can I name an "Eli" who I'm trying to impress with the way I worship?

- When I worship, what keeps me from putting everything else aside so I can focus on God?

- In what ways have I tried to steal God's glory?

- Who or what distracts me when I worship?

❖❖❖

Lord, I confess that I am easily distracted by the things of the world. Help me to focus my eyes on You.
Thank You, Father, that You are the Lord of glory and that You will give it to no one else. Show me Your glory, I pray. Help me turn aside, humble myself, and give You all the respect You deserve. Change my life the way You transformed the life of Moses. Teach me everything I need to know about what it means to truly worship You.

❖❖❖

The Real Deal

❖

God said to Moses, "I am who I am."

—Exodus 3:14

❖

ackson and I were kicking back. I was wearing jeans and a T-shirt, having a bad hair day, and wasn't wearing makeup. Jackson sprawled comfortably on my lap as I sat on the couch flipping through the TV channels. Nothing looked interesting, so I pushed the play button on the VCR remote, thinking one of Jackson's videos was in the player. Instead, the image of an impeccably dressed, superbly coiffed, perfectly made-up woman flashed on the screen.

"Mommy!" Jackson shouted.

There I was onstage speaking at a recent women's event.

When I tried to turn off the VCR, Jackson protested.

"No," he said, "I want to watch Mommy."

"You don't need to watch Mommy," I said. "She's right here." I pointed to myself to make sure he understood.

Jackson looked at me, then back at the screen. "No," he said, "I want *that* mommy!"

Jackson wanted the version of me he saw on the screen, even though at that moment he was sitting right on the lap of the real deal.

Isn't that the way we can be with God? We want the version of Him that corresponds to our ideas about what He is like or who we want Him to be. But to hear from God, we must know and accept Him as He really is. Our view of God becomes clearer when we recognize who we are in light of Him. Moses began to discover who God is by asking, "Who am I?"

WHO AM I?

When God chose to speak to Moses out of the burning bush, it was for a specific purpose. He had a plan for Moses' life, and He was about to tell Moses exactly how to start carrying it out. Once Moses had properly positioned himself to hear from God, the Lord spoke: "I am sending you to Pharaoh to bring my people the Israelites out of Egypt" (Exodus 3:10).

Whoa!

Moses had hid his face—now he wanted to hide the rest of his body! Though he had made the proper response to God's glory, he blew it when it came to obedience. "Who am I that I should go to Pharaoh and bring the Israelites out of Egypt?" he asked God.

Who am I for a job like that?

Whom shall I say sent me?

What if the Israelites don't believe me?

I can relate to how Moses felt when God told him what He wanted him to do. When my publisher first contacted me about writing this book, I felt so intimidated that as soon as my husband and I left the first meeting with the publishing team, I looked at him and exclaimed, "I can't do it!" I felt so ill-equipped for the task that I didn't even consider it. Jerry encouraged me to talk to the Lord before I made a decision.

Bible study and prayer convinced me that God wanted me to accept the challenge. But like Moses, I felt I would never measure up to the task. The Lord has had to continually remind me that He is in control and will accomplish good things through me. He wants to display His greatness through my inadequacy.

Moses' problem was that although he reverenced God, he didn't yet know Him very well. Understanding God's attributes—the distinguishing marks of His character—helps us appreciate Him in a deeper, more intimate way as it moves us from knowing about Him to truly knowing Him.

Because God is beyond our comprehension, what we know about Him can come in only one way: He must reveal it to us. So in response to each one of Moses' objections—lack of ability, lack of authority, and lack of credibility—God revealed an aspect of His character.

Instead of asking God, "Who am I?"
Moses should have asked Him,
"Who are You?"

Moses said to God, "Suppose I go to the Israelites and say to them, 'The God of your fathers has sent me to you,' and they ask me, 'What is his name?' Then what shall I tell them?" (Exodus 3:13).

"'This is what you are to say to the Israelites,'" God replied. "'I AM has sent me to you. . . . The LORD, the God of your fathers—the God of Abraham, the God of Isaac and the God of Jacob—has sent me to you'" (Exodus 3:14–15).

"I AM" is the name that expresses God's eternal faithfulness to His people. God wanted Moses to know that He never changes and that Moses could count on Him regardless of circumstances.

But Moses said: "'What if they do not believe me or listen to me and say, "The LORD did not appear to you"?'" (Exodus 4:1).

By now God was probably thinking that Moses was a visual learner, so to answer his question He showed him that He was the Lord over all creation. He empowered Moses to defy the laws of nature and perform three miraculous signs. In a dress rehearsal, God had Moses turn his staff into a serpent, make the flesh of his hand leprous, and then restore it. Then He said that if those weren't enough to convince the Israelites, Moses could take some water from the Nile River and turn it into blood (vv. 2–9).

Even after witnessing some of the miraculous signs God would enable him to perform, Moses still wasn't convinced he was the man for the job. "'O LORD,'" he said, "'I have never been eloquent, neither in the past nor since you have spoken to your servant. I am slow of speech and tongue'" (Exodus 4:10). God reminded Moses that He, the Creator, had made Moses' mouth and assured him that He Himself would go with Moses and teach him what to say.

When God tells you what He wants you to do, do you plead lack of authority, credibility, and ability? I often do. Though we, like Moses, should approach the presence of God with humility, we must not hang our heads because we feel unacceptable or inadequate. We must not end up saying, as Moses did, "O LORD, please send someone else to do it" (Exodus 4:13). God doesn't always call the equipped, but He always equips those He calls. He will never ask you to do something He won't enable you to accomplish. Instead of asking God, "Who am I?" Moses should have asked Him, "Who are You?"

WHO IS GOD?

To reassure Moses, God chose to reveal the things about Himself that Moses would need to know as he brought the children out of Egypt and led them through the wilderness. As I read the rest of Exodus, I discover that Moses remained dependent on God throughout his service to the Lord. He never thought he had arrived. Aware of his desperate need, Moses spent forty years with the Israelites in the wilderness getting to know God, and God responded by continuing to reveal His character.

God controls both how
He meets us and what He chooses
to reveal about Himself.

In Exodus 33:18, we find Moses' request of God: "Now show me your glory." The Lord's response appears in verses 19–23:

> And the LORD said, "I will cause all my goodness to pass in front of you, and I will proclaim my name, the LORD, in your presence. I will have mercy on whom I will have mercy, and I will have compassion on whom I will have compassion. But," he said, "you cannot see my face, for no one may see me and live."
>
> Then the LORD said, "There is a place near me where you may stand on a rock. When my glory passes by, I will put you in a cleft in the rock and cover you with my hand until I have passed by. Then I will remove my hand and you will see my back; but my face must not be seen."

Notice that God controlled how much of His glory Moses witnessed. No matter what we think we need, God controls both how He meets us and what He chooses to reveal about Himself. You may think you need His healing touch, while He may decide to reveal His peace in the midst of your ailing body. You may think you need His financial provision, but He may decide you need to learn that He is totally reliable. He knows what's best and will reveal what we need in His timing.

During their chat at the burning bush, God revealed to Moses what he needed to know to get started—that He is a faithful, all-powerful, always-present God. Though Moses had begun by asking "Who am I?" he would discover who God is *and* learn who God made him to be.

After Moses had led the children of Israel out of Egypt and was about to receive the second edition of the Ten Commandments at Mount Sinai, God showed up in person to remind him of His power and reveal two more of His attributes—His mercy and His justice.

God's Mercy

God told Moses that He was "the LORD, the LORD, the compassionate and gracious God, slow to anger, abounding in love and faithfulness" (Exodus 34:6). Have you ever wondered why God stressed His mercy just before He gave Moses the law?

God never gives law
without buffering it with grace.

I think God wanted to assure Moses that His mercy could extend even to people who have grumbled, rebelled, and worshiped idols. Remember that the Israelites had committed idolatry while Moses was on the mountain receiving God's commandments. With the people's great sin of creating and worshiping a golden calf fresh in his mind, Moses likely needed a reminder that God is great enough not only to defeat the Israelites' enemies, but also to forgive their iniquity.

In His mercy, God forgives sin, and no one is beyond His forgiveness. God never gives law without buffering it with grace. In the midst of our sin, He steps in and saves us from ourselves.

God's Justice

But Moses needed to know something else about God. After telling Moses that He is a God of mercy, God revealed that He is also a God of justice. To us, these attributes can seem mutually exclusive.

Remember Jackson's two mommies? Jackson couldn't see that the mommy on the couch and the mommy on the screen were the same person, so he focused on the one that appealed to him most. That's the way we are. We can't see how God's mercy and justice can both be true, so we focus on the one we like best. However, just as the real mommy was both the speaker onstage at a women's conference and the mommy on the couch at home, God's essence includes and expresses both mercy and justice.

In Exodus 34:7, God assures Moses that "he does not leave the guilty unpunished." Sin has consequences, and God punished the children of Israel for their idolatry. But although He punished the sin, He loved the sinners, and in His mercy He provided forgiveness.

Moses' response to God's revelation of His character appears in Exodus 34:8: "Moses bowed to the ground at once and worshiped." We don't know whether or not God revealed the attributes Moses felt he wanted to see, but Moses' actions show us he was satisfied with what he learned about God.

No matter how you feel, God's attributes remain true. God is the real deal, and His perfection sets Him apart from all others. Knowing His goodness makes us eager to obey.

GOD PLEASERS

I've already told you that humility was one of the things I struggled with as a preacher's kid. Another challenge was that I grew up trying to make sure I was pleasing everybody. The Lord had to show me that if I was going to worship Him the way He desired to be worshiped, I couldn't be worried about pleasing anybody else.

I know I'm not alone in this. In general, women have this bad, don't we? We want to make sure that everybody's taken care of and happy with us. Whenever you're tempted to focus on anything but God, go back to the book of Exodus and reread the descriptions of Moses' encounter with God at the burning bush.

Moses' conversation with God reveals that his concern was about how the Israelites would respond to him. Initially, this distracted him from seeing God clearly and worshiping Him accordingly. It made it difficult for him to hear what God was telling him. God revealed that Moses could carry out His instructions only if he took his eyes off the people and kept them on Him. If we are to hear clearly from God, we must do the same.

Undistracted worship develops intimacy with God, and intimacy with Him leads to increased communication with Him. If you want to hear from God, give Him the glory due Him by giving Him your single-minded worship.

WHERE ARE YOU NOW?

TAKE TIME FOR A GPS READING:

• When God tells me to do something that's difficult for me, how do I feel?

• What excuses have I given God for not doing what I know He's called me to do?

• How do I respond to revelations of God's glory?

• Am I more concerned with my response to God, or with people's response to me?

❖ ❖ ❖

Thank You, Father, that You are who You are.
I praise You for Your willingness to reveal everything
about Yourself that I need to know to do what You call me
to do. I confess that I often feel ill-equipped—in over my
head. Thank You for promising to work through me to
accomplish Your will. Help me not to worry about what
other people think so I will keep my focus on worshiping You.

❖ ❖ ❖

The Heart of the Matter

❖

These people come near to me with

their mouth and honor me with their lips,

but their hearts are far from me.

—Isaiah 29:13

❖

Jackson's dedication service took place in January 2003. Baby dedications at our church are a *really* big deal. The babies and their families and friends are presented to the entire church, so I planned everything down to the last detail.

For several weeks beforehand I dressed little Jackson in several of his cutest outfits and parted his hair on one side and then the other, mentally gauging which combination was best. By the time the big day arrived, everything was perfect. My baby was adorable, my husband was handsome, and my ensemble was flawless. I was so excited as we set out from home that morning. Most of our congregation was going to see my son for the first time!

But as we drove to the church, a weight hit my spirit. In planning my son's event, I had considered every detail and person except the most important—the Lord. In focusing on external appearances, I had forgotten that the purpose of the event was to worship God by dedicating Jackson to Him. Embarrassment and shame filled me. I was so focused on impressing people that I had forgotten the heart of the matter—worshiping God.

IT'S NOT ABOUT US

If you're like most women, you've probably gone to church and been so concerned with the shoes you had on, the clothes you were wearing, or the people you were going to see when you got there that you forgot that church isn't supposed to be about us. What is the real reason we do what we do? Are we worshiping God for His glory or for our own? Is our goal to turn eyes to Him or toward us?

We need to take close inventory of our hearts to make sure our motives for worship are pure. John 4:24 describes the type of worshiper God seeks: "God is spirit, and his worshipers must worship in spirit and in truth."

Deuteronomy 4:29 says that when we search for the Lord with all of our hearts we will find Him. So what keeps us from clearly hearing His voice? Maybe our heart is the core of the problem. To be single-minded in our search for God, our hearts cannot be caught up in anything that steals attention from Him. The Lord is not impressed with our seemingly religious activities and halfhearted approaches to worship. He is concerned with whether the search for Him finds root in the heart. It's all about priorities.

GOD'S PRIORITIES

Recently my home church leadership sought to make some changes. Our pastor explained that the goal was to honor God and invite Him to move powerfully in our fellowship. One Sunday the pastor made a statement I will never forget. He said, "A focus on divine order always precedes an infilling of God's divine presence." When we want God to reveal Himself to us, we need to make the things that are important to Him our priorities as well.

> *God wants the worship of those who are*
> *willingly present and centered on Him.*

When God calls us, He always calls us for a specific purpose. The reason God called Moses is found in Exodus 9:1: "Go to Pharaoh and say to him, 'This is what the LORD, the God of the Hebrews, says: Let my people go *so that they may worship me.*'" God brought the Israelites out of Egypt so that they could bring Him glory by worshiping Him. That was His priority, and His plans were based on it.

Once the Israelites had been freed from their captivity, God told Moses to build a tabernacle of worship so He would meet with them there. He was very specific about who was to build the temple and how they were to build it.

The Israelites were all God's people, but He wanted only those whose hearts were stirred to participate in this project—like those who brought freewill offerings morning after morning in gratitude to God (Exodus 25:2; 36:3). God wants the worship of those who are willingly present and centered on Him.

God also gave specific instructions about the tabernacle itself and everything in it—the furniture, linens, curtains, pillars, beams, and decor. Imagine the time and patience required to meet each specification! Everything had to be done correctly, for the temple was to be a holy place where God would dwell among His people (Exodus 25:8). It was the place where He would speak to them (v. 22).

God knew that the Israelites couldn't make it a priority to worship Him single-mindedly while they were being held in bondage in Egypt. They couldn't be devoted to Him while they were slaves to

Pharaoh. They didn't have enough time and energy to do both well. But once God brought His people out of Egypt, they were free to serve Him with all their hearts. And when they did, when they took God's priorities seriously and followed His plans, He invited them into His very presence and made His will known to them.

Are you serving the Lord wholeheartedly? Are you focused on His priorities and His plans? If not, the reason could be that you're still in bondage. The question is this: What's still holding you captive?

IN BONDAGE TO PHARAOH

There are so many things that can hold us women captive. I call these things "pharaohs." We can be enslaved by the pharaohs of religious boundaries, the need to please, a relationship, or even comparing ourselves to one another. If you're in bondage to a pharaoh of any kind, God wants to free you so you can worship Him with all your heart. I'd like to give you three examples of pharaohs in my own life and tell you how God in His mercy freed me from their bondage so I could worship Him with single-minded devotion.

The Pharaoh of Past Mistakes

Freeway 59 North cuts right through Houston, Texas. While I was an undergraduate there, that freeway took me many places—including some places I shouldn't have been. I took one particular exit off 59 North a lot, and it came to symbolize one of the most emotionally difficult times of my life. Although I haven't lived in Houston since I graduated, just the thought of that exit brings to mind events that changed my life forever and left me with a scar too great for me to deal with on my own.

A couple of years ago I visited Houston to speak at a women's event. On the way from the airport to my hotel, my hosts' car turned onto 59 North, and suddenly my thoughts took me back to my place of hurt. As the car drove onward toward the exit that served as a painful reminder of my past, my eyes filled with tears. There I sat, years removed from the events that had scarred me, yet unable to control my emotional response to the visual reminder of my pain. My thoughts raced and my heart ached.

And then . . . we passed the exit. Suddenly it was behind us, and I heard the Master's voice speak clearly to me: *Priscilla, wipe away your tears. That road is behind you now. You have passed the exit of your shame, and you are beyond the pain that accompanied it. I have many other roads ahead for you.*

As I wiped away my tears, it dawned on me that I had never ventured on this part of 59 North. I had never gone farther than that exit. For the first time, I was traveling beyond it and seeing parts of Houston I had never seen before. In the same way, the Lord was allowing me to go to a place spiritually further than I ever had gone so I could see things about His grace and will for my life. I had never seen these things before because I hadn't moved past my deepest hurt. I rejoiced that the very same road that had been my pathway to sin was now leading me to a work for the Lord.

> *One of the best things you can do to worship God single-mindedly is simply to accept where you are and what He's doing for you right now.*

I sat in the backseat of that car and basked in the love of our great God, who is willing to restore us and remind us that there is a road beyond our hurt. There is a path beyond our shame. There is an exit off of the freeway of our worst memory that will lead us right to the abundant, spectacular will of God.

Sister, if you are in bondage to the pharaoh of past mistakes, here is the Lord's Word to you today: "Forget the former things; do not dwell on the past. See, I am doing a new thing! Now it springs up; do you not perceive it?" (Isaiah 43:18–19).

The Pharaoh of Present Frustrations

Several months ago, I was out jogging in my neighborhood early in the morning, and to be honest with you, I was frustrated at the prospect of another day at home with the kids, wiping noses and picking up toys. I was just tired of taking care of everybody, you know? And as I jogged through the neighborhood, I was complaining about it under my breath.

As I neared an intersection, a car drove right past me, and a lady I didn't know stuck her head out the window and yelled, "Hallelujah!" I have no idea what made her want to say that. All I know is that when she said it, the Holy Spirit reminded me that there's always something to praise God for. In the midst of what you are going through, no matter how frustrated you feel with your circumstances, there is always some reason for you to worship God. He says there's something for you to praise Him about right now.

One of the best things you can do to worship God single-mindedly is simply to accept where you are and what He's doing for you *right now*. Be alert. Be present. Don't miss out on what God is doing.

Sister, if you are in bondage to the pharaoh of present frustrations, here is the Lord's Word to you today: "God is able to make all grace abound to you, so that in all things at all times, having all that you need, you will abound in every good work" (2 Corinthians 9:8).

The Pharaoh of Future Anxiety

I had thought and prayed about that day all of my life, and now it had finally arrived. I was engaged to be married to a man I loved with all my heart. I actually had a ring on my finger, and it wasn't a piece of cosmetic jewelry that I had bought myself. This one was real . . . and it was from a real man! But now that the big day was approaching, I felt . . . well . . . kind of weird. I wondered why I wasn't jumping out of my skin with excitement and joy.

For two or three months as the excitement mounted before my engagement, I had asked advice from everyone I thought had any kind of spiritual qualifications at all. Do you think I'm ready for marriage? Do you think that Jerry is the one? Do you think there's anything at all I might want to consider before making this big decision?

The butterflies in my stomach were flying in so many different directions that I was sure they must all have concussions from running into each other. I thought that maybe some profound statement from a friend would at least make those butterflies fly in formation. But nothing anyone said really made any kind of sense or made me feel any better. Anxiety was taking its toll on me, and I felt all alone.

Worry is not only fruitless, but it steals our joy and jams our radar, keeping us from receiving the answers we need.

Now I know that my anxiety was the Lord telling me that what He wanted was for me to seek Him first. There is only one who can lead us in the right direction when we need answers to life's biggest questions. You know who it is. Why not just go to Him first, instead of waiting until anxiety has you at your wit's end? Worry is not only fruitless, but it steals our joy and jams our radar, keeping us from receiving the answers we need. God wants to lead us in every area of our lives, but He waits for us to come to Him.

As you have no doubt guessed, I finally decided to allow God to take control of my relationship with Jerry, and we were married on July 24, 1999.

Sister, if you are in bondage to the pharaoh of future anxiety, here is the Lord's Word to you today: "Do not be anxious about anything, but in everything, by prayer and petition, with thanksgiving, present your requests to God" (Philippians 4:6).

YOU'RE NOT IN EGYPT ANYMORE

My pharaohs have taught me that to worship God wholeheartedly, I have to get out of Egypt and stay out of Egypt. My favorite verse in the Bible is Galatians 5:1: "It is for freedom that Christ has set us free. Stand firm, then, and do not let yourselves be burdened again by a yoke of slavery." I encourage you to repeat this verse aloud using the personal pronoun "me." Write it on a card and post it on your bathroom mirror, car dashboard, or somewhere else you will see it often.

One of the great riches you inherited when you accepted Christ's death on Calvary was freedom. You've been released. You no longer are enslaved. In the Old Testament, God sent Moses to declare freedom to His people. In the New Testament He sent His Son, Jesus. He declares to you and me today that we are *free*.

One day it dawned on me that I wasn't really sure why the children of Israel were in captivity in the first place. I never knew how they got there, so I did a little Bible reading. Exodus 1:8–10 is very clear about why they were there. It says that the pharaoh at the time was becoming intimidated. He looked at those Jews growing in number and power, and he was scared. So he enslaved the Hebrews so that they wouldn't overpower him.

Listen, my friend, the only reason you're still in captivity is because the Enemy is intimidated. The Bible says that God inhabits the praises of His people. Satan doesn't want you praising God because he doesn't want God to show up in your life. He knows that if you ever break free from whatever is keeping you captive, you'll worship God with wholehearted devotion and begin to hear His voice. And when a woman hears God's voice and obeys Him, she's powerful.

WHERE ARE YOU NOW?

TAKE TIME FOR A GPS READING:

• What is my true motive for worship?

• How do I know that I am giving God the authentic worship He desires?

• What is my main priority in life?

• What am I in bondage to that keeps me from hearing from God?

❖ ❖ ❖

Thank You, Father, for showing us what matters most to
You. I want my motives to be pure. I want Your priorities
to be my priorities, and I want Your glory to be the reason
for everything I do. Help me grasp the freedom that is
mine in Christ so that I can move beyond the pain of the
past, rejoice amid the frustrations of the present, and lay
my anxiety about the future at Your feet.

❖ ❖ ❖

PART THREE

A Set-Apart Holiness

The word of the Lord was rare in those days;
there was no widespread revelation.

—1 Samuel 3:1 NKJV

❖

The third characteristic that positioned Samuel to hear
from God was a *set-apart holiness*. Believers in Jehovah God
were not hearing much from Him in Samuel's day. So if
Samuel was one of the chosen few who heard from God,
it must mean that he somehow stood out from the crowd.
While the people around him were tolerating sin, Samuel
was determined to live a life that was holy before God.

When God Is Silent

❖

There is a time for everything, and

a season for every activity under heaven . . .

a time to be silent and a time to speak.

—Ecclesiastes 3:1, 7

❖

"I've heard from God," he said.

He was an outspoken homosexual up for election as a bishop in the Episcopal Church. On a nationally broadcast television show with an audience of thousands, this man insisted that God approved of his homosexual lifestyle and endorsed his position as a church leader. I listened as he claimed that he had the ability to judge between the voice in his own head and God's voice. "My decision," he said of his plan to become a bishop, "is certainly one based on the voice of God."

I sat in stunned shock as I watched, horrified by his declaration that God had supposedly given the thumbs-up to both his lifestyle and his ambition to hold church office. Scripture makes it very clear not only that this man's lifestyle violates God's requirements for holy living but also that He withholds His voice from those who consistently indulge in sin.

SIN CLOSES GOD'S MOUTH

The second half of 1 Samuel 3:1 tells us that "the word of the LORD was rare." Neither the children of Israel nor their leaders were hearing God speak, not even those who said they believed in Yahweh and followed Him.

It bothers me that the Jewish people, who claimed to have a relationship with Yahweh, weren't hearing His voice. It kind of sounds like the body of Christ today, doesn't it? We Christians aren't used to hearing God. Case in point: Aren't we sometimes taken aback when believers boldly claim they've heard the voice of God? Why should that be so shocking? We should be used to hearing God speak. But we're not, and neither was the nation of Israel in Samuel's day.

The children of Israel had heard *God's Word, but they had chosen not to* listen, *and so God finally quit speaking to them.*

In chapter 1, we saw that one of the reasons God chose to speak to Samuel was that he was willing to listen. Samuel's listening involved not merely attentively hearing, but also anticipation to respond in obedience. Most Israelites had been ignoring or rebelling against God for years. From the day He brought them out of Egypt, they had begun forsaking Him and serving other gods (1 Samuel 8:8).

So God said to them, "The days are coming . . . when I will send a famine through the land—not a famine of food or a thirst for water, but a famine of hearing the words of the LORD" (Amos 8:11). The children of Israel had *heard* God's Word, but they had chosen not to *listen,* and so God finally quit speaking to them. His silence had overshadowed Israel for many years, but He was about to speak again. And when He did, He spoke to a young boy whose holy lifestyle set him apart from the crowd.

It still bothers me that God didn't speak to Eli. If there was anyone who should have heard from Him, it was the high priest. As a Levite, Eli had a very godly lineage, and he was a judge over Israel for forty years. The Israelites looked to him as the mediator between them and God and turned to him for spiritual, economic, and even civil instruction. Their blessing came from this man. Yet God didn't choose to speak to the high priest. A quick overview of 1 Samuel 2 tells us why.

Eli was a good man, but his sons Hophni and Phineas were wicked, and he let them get totally out of control. They were demanding the best part of worshipers' offerings for themselves and even seducing the women who served at the entrance to the tabernacle. Eli heard about what his sons were doing and rebuked them, but that was all he did. He didn't use the power that was his as high priest to stop them, even after God sent him a message that He was going to cut off Eli's family line of priests for dishonoring Him (1 Samuel 2:27–36).

Eli was tolerating sin. Yes, he had a godly background, he had the status, and he had the title—but he also had sin in his life. What does Eli's story tell us? It tells us that background doesn't set us apart. It tells us that status or titles don't set us apart. It tells us that age doesn't set us apart. Even knowledge of God's Word doesn't set us apart, for Eli certainly knew a whole lot more Scripture than twelve-year-old Samuel. Allowing the Holy Spirit to work in us is what sets us apart. The apostle Paul told Titus that Jesus Christ "gave his life to free us from every kind of sin, to cleanse us and to make us his very own people, totally committed to doing what is right" (Titus 2:14 NLT). Samuel was set apart to God because he was totally committed to doing what was right, and it showed in the way he lived his life.

He shone like a bright light against the background of the darkness around him.

Paul explains what happens to people who have a head knowledge of God but refuse to honor Him with their lives by obeying Him: "Although they knew God, they neither glorified him as God nor gave thanks to him, but their thinking became futile and their foolish hearts were darkened. Although they claimed to be wise, they became fools" (Romans 1:21–22).

That seems to be what happened to Hophni and Phineas. They certainly knew God—Eli would have seen to that—but they did not revere Him. In fact, they were so wicked that Eli feared them more than he reverenced the Lord. Part of the message God gave Samuel was that Eli's sons would die because of their sins.

Christians who don't hear from God should be on the lookout for unconfessed sin and rebellion in their lives. Now, don't get me wrong. God isn't looking for a sinless people. He knows there aren't any. He's just looking for a people who are serious about hearing His Word and obeying it. Is the Holy Spirit bringing to your mind an area of life in which you have refused to obey God? If so, don't ignore it. Acknowledge it and confess it so you can get on with the business of creating an intimate relationship with the Father.

While Eli was tolerating sin, Samuel was determined to live a life that was righteous before God. While Eli and his sons were busy sinning, Samuel was busy obeying God. This is what set him apart to God and opened his ears to hear His voice.

SILENCE OPENS OUR EARS

Sometimes we are living a holy life, but we still don't hear God's voice. When that happens, we can become angry with Him. We expect that since we have finally obeyed, He will reward us by speaking immediately and clearly, but that isn't necessarily the way He shows us that He is God.

He is not only the God who divides the Red Sea of our problems. He is not only the God who makes the walls of our Jerichos fall down. Although He is more than able to intervene, sometimes He shows His glory, demonstrates His power, and strengthens His children by His silence.

Matthew tells the story of a Canaanite woman who called out to Jesus as He and His disciples were traveling. The woman begged Jesus to have mercy on her daughter, who was "suffering terribly from demon-possession" (Matthew 15:22). Jesus, however, didn't say a word. He just kept walking (v. 23).

I wonder how that poor woman felt. She was calling out to God with all of her might, looking for a solution to her problem, trying to get this God who claimed to love her to help her in her situation. Yet the Master said nothing and did nothing. He was silent. Tired of hearing this persistent woman call out to Jesus, the disciples traveling with Him urged Him to do something for her so she would go away.

The disciples were interested in solving a physical problem, while the Messiah was interested in teaching a spiritual lesson. I have found that in our frailty we are almost always concerned with physical solutions to our problems, while in His deity, God is concerned with teaching us far more important spiritual lessons.

Undeterred by the Master's silence, the Canaanite woman continued to beg Him for help. He gave her a reason for not helping her (v. 24). She ignored it. He insulted her (v. 26). It didn't matter. She didn't care what the reason was or what others thought of her. She just kept coming. She fell down before the Lord, willing to accept whatever He would give. Anything would do as long as it came from her Lord. Finally, Jesus answered: "Woman, you have great faith! Your request is granted" (v. 28). And the daughter of that faithful woman was healed.

I believe that this woman left with more than what she had begged God for. She left the presence of the Master knowing more about the silence of God. When she received no response, she bowed lower to the ground. She humbled herself further and persisted in her request. I wonder if she would have been as humble and persevering a believer if she had received an immediate response. God's silence increased the

intensity of her pursuit. And that is exactly what God wants most—
not to merely give us want we want but to cause us to want Him more.
It is in wanting God that we get what He wants for us.

God is using silence to strengthen
your trust in Him and open
your ears to spiritual truths.

We know that we are becoming spiritually mature when God is
silent and, instead of asking why, we humble ourselves before Him
and persevere in prayer. It is a mark of maturity to believe that even
though God may be silent, He is still in control.

Are you calling out to the silent Jesus right now for a solution to
a problem you face, yet you are frustrated because He isn't answering you in the clear, loud way you had hoped? Pursue the Savior! Pay
no attention to those who are watching and wishing you would just
give it up already.

Trust that in His silence, God *is* speaking to you. He wants silence
to make you desperate not for a solution to your problem, but for
more of Him. God is using silence to strengthen your trust in Him
and open your ears to spiritual truths.

God knows when it's time to speak and when it's time to keep
silent. If He has chosen to leave you in the situation you're in, on your
knees and listening for Him, there's a reason, although more often
than not He doesn't tell us what it is. Sometimes He just watches and
waits to see what our next move will be—to see if we will obey the
commands of His Word.

A GARBLED MESSAGE

Without a standard to gauge our communication with God, you
and I can easily fall into error about what He directs us to do. We
can easily be fooled into thinking He has spoken to us or to others

when He hasn't. We must remember that God's spoken word never contradicts His written Word. Individuals who "hear from God" without taking time to verify the message against Scripture risk falling into grave error.

We are imperfect humans trying to hear from a perfect God. Even the most well-intentioned individuals who desire to obey God can misunderstand His instructions. The problem is not with God's communication skills; the problem is with our ability to listen clearly. You could compare us to satellite dishes that collect signals to provide clear television reception. Sometimes environmental conditions can interfere with the reception and affect the ability to provide clear pictures.

Likewise, many things in our lives can interfere with our ability to receive God's messages, things such as having too much to do and too many distractions. Many things clamor for our attention when life gets busy, and hearing God's voice in the midst of the chaos can be difficult. The biggest jamming device, however, is sin. Sin scrambles our reception of God's messages by diminishing our ability to receive strong spiritual signals.

Scripture descrambles the message by either authenticating or disproving what we think we've heard. As we seek God's direction and listen for His reply, we must verify that the voice we hear in response is God's and not our own, much less that of Satan. How can we be sure that other voices aren't drowning out God's? We must learn to discern the truth based on the principles in Scripture.

God's absolute standards are revealed only in His Word, and we need to recognize that only the Bible is absolute truth. God will never give us fresh words that contradict His written Word. In looking at why God didn't speak to Eli and his sons, we looked at Romans 1:21–22, which explains what happens to people who have a head knowledge of God but refuse to honor Him. The rest of the passage tells us where this can lead:

> Therefore God gave them over in the sinful desires of their
> hearts to sinful impurity for the degrading of their bodies

with one another. They exchanged the truth of God for a
lie. . . . Because of this, God gave them over to shameful
lusts . . . [and] men abandoned natural relations with women
and were inflamed with lust for one another. Men committed
indecent acts with other men, and received in themselves
the due penalty for their perversion. (vv. 24–27)

The Bible doesn't call homosexuality an alternative lifestyle—it
calls it sin (Leviticus 18:22; Romans 13:13; 1 Corinthians 6:9–10;
1 Timothy 1:9–10). So we can be sure that the would-be bishop did
not hear from God. Although God can and does remain silent at times
to strengthen believers, He usually only speaks to those with persistent sin in their lives to warn them of His coming judgment and convince them of their need to repent.

That was God's message to Eli, but sin jammed the priest's receiving apparatus, and he didn't get the message. In fact, sin often
prevented the entire nation of Israel from hearing from God. Although Eli had ignored God's first warning, God wanted him to hear
it again. So He looked around for someone whose walk was holy to
speak to—and He found Samuel, set apart and ready to listen.

WHERE ARE YOU NOW?

❖

TAKE TIME FOR A GPS READING:

- How often do I hear the Word of God but don't really listen?

- What aspects of my lifestyle would cause others to conclude that I am set apart to God?

- What has been my response when God has answered my prayers with silence?

- Have I made any lifestyle choices that don't conform to God's Word? If so, what are they?

❖ ❖ ❖

Father God, I confess that You know exactly when to speak and when to keep silent. If Your silence will convict me of my sin, I thank You for Your silence. If Your silence will make me more like You, I thank You for Your silence. If Your silence will cause me to pursue You more passionately, I thank You for Your silence. Teach me to trust You so much that I will no longer doubt You. Help me hold up every message I receive to the mirror of Your Word so that I can know when it is truly from You.

❖ ❖ ❖

Perfecting Holiness

❖

Since we have these promises, dear friends,

let us purify ourselves from everything

that contaminates body and spirit,

perfecting holiness out of reverence for God.

—2 Corinthians 7:1

❖

In 1956, a little band of missionaries in Ecuador hoped to share the gospel with the Auca Indian tribe. They had established a good relationship with the tribe, but one day when Jim Elliot and four other missionaries went to visit them, the Indians speared all five men to death. One of the men who participated in the killing went by the name of Grandfather. I had heard about this event all of my life, but several years ago I heard Grandfather speak, and what he said changed my life forever.

Grandfather told us that Christ was now his Savior and that he and his tribesmen were serving Him. They had taken their place as sons and daughters of the King, and they were living lives that demonstrated their new identity in the Lord. He said that he was shocked at how Christians in America seem to so closely resemble the rest of secular society, and he was dismayed that they weren't living in a way that clearly showed they served a different God.

The Holy Spirit pinned me to my chair and convicted me: Christ's life in us should make us different. We're no longer supposed to act like pagans. How can we expect God to speak to us when we act the same as we did before we knew Him? Just like Grandfather's tribe, we must choose to live sanctified lives that set us apart from the world.

ALIENS AND STRANGERS

The Bible says that we're supposed to be aliens and strangers in this world. We're supposed to be a very special people, set apart to God. In Scripture, to be "set apart" is to be *sanctified* and *holy*.

There are three stages of sanctification. The first, *positional sanctification* (also called justification) happens when we accept God's gift of salvation through the great work of Christ on the cross. Positional sanctification frees us from the *penalty of sin*, and it's the result of what Christ did. When we accept that Christ died for our sins, God immediately declares us righteous, and our new standing before Him never changes. Once we have been positionally sanctified, we become a part of God's family, and He will speak to us because of that relationship.

The second stage of sanctification is *lifestyle sanctification*. Lifestyle sanctification frees us from the *power of sin*, and this requires our participation. It involves a decision on our part to allow the Holy Spirit to work in us so we can live a life that pleases our heavenly Father. When we make that decision, we get close to Him and can hear His voice.

Finally, there is *ultimate sanctification*, or glorification. This will occur when God frees us from the *presence of sin* and we don't have to worry about it anymore. We won't experience this kind of sanctification until we meet the Lord face-to-face.

After accepting Christ as Savior, we're concerned with lifestyle sanctification—the process by which you and I, day after day and moment by moment, become more and more like Christ. Although we have been positionally sanctified by faith in Christ, it's our responsibility to actively pursue lifestyle sanctification by yielding to the power of God's Spirit in us. We cannot live a lifestyle of perpetually unrepentant sin and expect to hear God's voice. The two cannot coexist.

Let me warn you, lifestyle sanctification isn't particularly easy, necessarily convenient, or especially fun. You have to make a decision to pursue it regardless of the way it feels, because I can tell you right now that it isn't going to be the most enjoyable thing you've ever done in your life.

> *The closer and more intimate your relationship with God becomes, the more clearly you are going to hear Him speak.*

When I was growing up, we went to Six Flags a lot. At that particular theme park, there are signs that tell you how long you'll have to wait before you get on a ride. If the sign says "two hours from this point," it means you'll have to stand in line under the hot Texas sun for at least that long. Nevertheless, we and three hundred other crazy people would stand in line for two hours to take a ride that lasted two minutes. We stood there because we believed the ride was going to be worth it.

That's the same reason we should persevere in living a holy life. Lifestyle sanctification will require us to make hard choices and to do what is right in order to bring honor to God. Yes, it's going to be difficult sometimes. It's often going to be like the hot Texas sun beating down on us. But the ride will be worth it. And it will last a whole lot longer than two minutes!

When you commit yourself to live a sanctified life, you may be the only mom in your neighborhood who chooses not to gossip about the others; you may be the only self-employed woman who chooses not to cheat on her taxes; you may be the only single woman at the party who chooses to save physical intimacy for marriage. If so, you will be different, and I guarantee you'll stick out. You'll be an alien and a stranger in this world, and that means you may be lonely sometimes. So the question is this: Is what you'll gain worth it to you?

A DOUBLE INCENTIVE

The apostle Paul understood what it meant to be set apart to God, and he had a great deal to say about sanctification. One of his clearest teachings on lifestyle sanctification appears in his letters to the Corinthians.

When Paul wrote his first letter to the Corinthians, he addressed it to "the church of God in Corinth, to those sanctified in Christ" (1 Corinthians 1:2). Paul was obviously referring to the Corinthian believers' positional sanctification, since the rest of the letter makes it clear that their lives were definitely not set apart. In fact, the Corinthians are one of the least godly groups of believers mentioned in Scripture.

Let me give you a little background on Corinth. The city had a lot in common with America—it was famous for its wealth and trade but also infamous for its immorality. The description "Corinthian woman" was the proverbial phrase for a prostitute. To "play the Corinthian" meant to act like a harlot. However, in the midst of all Corinth's lewdness, a small church was growing, and Paul wrote to the new believers to urge them to make their actions match up with their set-apart position. "Let us purify ourselves from everything that contaminates body and spirit," he wrote, "perfecting holiness out of reverence for God" (2 Corinthians 7:1).

Paul knew that choosing to live holy lives would be difficult for the Corinthians, so he gave them some incentives. These incentives will also encourage us in the choices we make to set ourselves apart to God. Back up a couple of verses and you'll see what they are. The first is found in 2 Corinthians 6:16, where Paul writes, "God has said, 'I will dwell with them and walk among them.'" Do you see the trade-off? The first incentive for living a sanctified life is fellowship with the Most High. The closer and more intimate your relationship with God becomes, the more clearly you are going to hear Him speak. While you might not have fellowship with everyone around you, you will have fellowship with your God.

> *Some want the distinction*
> *of being Christians without*
> *the difference of being holy.*

Paul also gives us the incentive of having a special relationship with God. "'Therefore come out from them and be separate,'" says the Lord. "'Touch no unclean thing, and I will receive you. I will be a Father to you, and you will be my sons and daughters'" (vv. 17–18). What Paul is saying here is that your positional sanctification in Christ should make you want to bring God glory with your lifestyle. The fact is that He has adopted you into His family. You are His daughter.

Do you understand that God didn't *have* to do that? In His grace and mercy, He *chose* to do that. That should be all the incentive we need to glorify God with our lives. Through the indwelling of the Holy Spirit, our Father has graciously given us the power we need to keep from indulging in sin, so we should be serious and persistent about living a life that pleases Him. As part of His family, we are representatives of Him.

When I was young, Daddy always told us kids to remember our last name. He wanted us to act like his children and leave people with a good impression of our family. My mother's advice, probably because I look so much like her, was even more specific: "Do not go anywhere or do anything questionable, because people might mistake you for me!"

I was positionally "set apart" to my parents because I was and always would be their child. However, they also demanded that I live as a positive testimony to the Evans's name. My parents trusted me to act in a way that positively distinguished me as their daughter, not just for my sake but also for theirs.

As believers, we've been born into the family of God, and His family name has a holy reputation. We are His children, and we must choose a lifestyle that doesn't jeopardize that great heritage. Daily, we must make decisions that are different from the world's. When I was younger and would leave the house by myself, my parents would say, "Priscilla, remember your last name. You're an Evans, so act like it." Paul tells us to remember our last name. We're saints, so let's act like it.

A DISTINCTION WITHOUT A DIFFERENCE

I wonder if we generally opt out of a holy lifestyle because we want to blend in with the crowd. Some want the distinction of being Christians without the difference of being holy.

I've met believers who have a very conservative view of what it means to live a set-apart life. Sometimes I've looked at them and thought, *Man, you mean you can't even do* that? But then later I've wondered if I've watered down the truth of what holiness really is because I'd rather blend in than stick out like a sore thumb. I've gone to parties and laughed at the jokes or just sat in silence and done nothing when I should have said or done something, anything, to show that I was a Christian and that I was different. I've been one of the Christians that Grandfather was worried about. How about you?

You and I are no longer pagans. We've been called to set ourselves apart from this world, and it's time for us to walk in a manner worthy of our calling. Only then can we experience the intimacy that brings increased communication with our God. By being holy, we prepare ourselves to hear our holy God speak. As we cooperate with the Holy Spirit to set ourselves apart in holiness out of our love and reverence for Jesus, we build a relationship with Him that will enable us to more clearly hear His voice.

WHERE ARE YOU NOW?

❖

TAKE TIME FOR A GPS READING:

• What would Grandfather say if he followed me around for a day?

• What things have I done that I think might have embarrassed God?

• How important to me are God's incentives for living a sanctified life?

• In what ways have I tried to blend in so I wouldn't stick out as different?

❖ ❖ ❖

Father, I thank You so much that You have made me Your daughter. Thank You that in Your great mercy You adopted me into Your family and that I can have fellowship with You. I want to honor our family name in all that I do. Lord, You know how hard it is for me to live a set-apart life. Help me rely on the incredible power of the Holy Spirit. I know that I will hear You speak to me on earth—and I look forward to seeing You face-to-face in heaven.

❖ ❖ ❖

Running to Win

❖

I have finished the race,

I have kept the faith.

Now there is in store for me

the crown of righteousness.

—2 Timothy 4:7–8

❖

When I was in high school, I was part of the track-and-field team. Before a race, all of us would run a warm-up lap around the arena. We would have on our heavy sweats and tennis shoes because we wanted to make sure that our muscles were warmed up for the race. But when we got ready to race, we took off those sweats and put on some lightweight shoes called spikes. We got rid of the excess baggage because we wanted to win races.

To win the race of the Christian life, we have to get serious about holiness, and that means getting rid of the baggage. For me this means not watching certain television shows and not reading certain books. It means getting out of certain relationships. Some friendships with good people have had to go because they weren't moving me toward the finish line by spurring me on in my relationship with Christ. When you're just warming up or having fun, you can take the baggage. But when you're running for a prize, when you want to cross that finish line and hear "well done," you simply have to get rid of everything that weighs you down.

EYES ON THE PRIZE

In 2 Corinthians 6, Paul tells us why we should pursue a lifestyle of sanctification. In the following chapter he tells us how. He tells us to "purify ourselves from everything that contaminates body and spirit." *The Message* translates this verse: "Make a clean break from everything that distracts you." I love that.

Satan knows that once you're a believer, he can't destroy you, so he's just out to distract you. He knows he can't get you for eternity, so he just wants to make sure you're no good for the kingdom of God while you're here on earth. He knows he can't keep you out of the race, but he'll do whatever it takes to see that you don't get the prize.

Coach Paul, however, cheers you on from the sidelines:

> Run in such a way as to get the prize. Everyone who competes in the games goes into strict training. They do it to get a crown that will not last; but we do it to get a crown that will last forever. Therefore I do not run like a man running aimlessly; I do not fight like a man beating the air. No, I beat my body and make it my slave so that after I have preached to others, I myself will not be disqualified for the prize. (1 Corinthians 9:24–27)

Running to win means dying to the flesh by not letting sin reign in your body (Romans 6:12). As Christians, we have a responsibility to die to the flesh daily, to let go of those things that distract us from our relationship with the Lord. For me, gluttony is a sin that is a constant struggle. I love to eat! It makes me happy to see good food waiting for me. I'm not one of those women who are happy to order a little salad. I'll not only devour the meat and potatoes on my own plate, but I'll also scan yours for leftovers and eat those too if you let me.

The world's freedom can become a slavery
that leads to emptiness and despair.

God has dealt with me on this. Every day I must die to my desire to eat more than I need. I'm not always successful, but I know that denying myself the extra helpings will ultimately make me a better example of how God's children should live. As I get more into the habit of sacrificing my selfish desires in this area, it becomes easier. But I suspect that gluttony will always be a struggle for me.

You may not identify with my particular temptation, but unless you are chiseled from granite, you have to deal with your own. What sins do you have to crucify daily? It helps to call them by the same name the Bible does. Notice I didn't say that I have a healthy appetite; I said that I have a problem with gluttony. Just like me, you need to know what tempts you to sin and be intentional about dealing with it.

FREE TO CHOOSE

We can deal with our temptations because, thanks be to God, we are no longer under sin's power. Paul assures us that Jesus has set us free: "We know that our old self was crucified with him so that the body of sin might be done away with, that we should no longer be slaves to sin" (Romans 6:6).

The world's freedom can encourage the choice for open rebellion against God. But that kind of freedom carries a heavy price. Sexual freedom leads to guilt, sickness, and unwanted pregnancy. The freedom to abuse chemical substances results in addiction and isolation. Freedom to gossip leads to distrust and broken relationships. The world's freedom can become a slavery that leads to emptiness and despair. God's freedom, on the other hand, leads to abundance and peace.

A life yielded to God results in the fruit of the Spirit: love, joy, peace, patience, kindness, goodness, faithfulness, gentleness, and self-control (Galatians 5:22–23). As Christians, we must embrace our freedom from sin. Paul tells us that we must make choices that will lead us to live lives set apart to God:

> Do not let sin reign in your mortal body so that you obey its lusts, and do not go on presenting the members of your body to sin as instruments of unrighteousness; but present yourselves to God as those alive from the dead, and your members as instruments of righteousness to God. (Romans 6:12–13 NASB)

In this passage, the words *let, obey,* and *present* are actions that require a choice. The world makes dying daily to the flesh a great challenge. To meet it, whenever we are tempted to sin, we must ask ourselves: *To what do I choose to yield—to my flesh or to God?*

Okay, let's say you've made your choice. You've signed up for the race, Jesus has paid your entrance fee, and you've memorized the rule book. You're determined to run this race God's way and win that prize.

Ready! You're on the track.

Set! You're in the block.

Go! You're . . . flat on your face.

What happened? You forgot to get rid of the sweats and put on the spikes.

You see, lifestyle sanctification doesn't stop with a choice. Sanctification means dying to the flesh, but it also means living to Christ.

We must be set apart *from* one thing and set apart *to* something else. Paul tells us this means putting off some things and putting on others. We are to put off anger, rage, malice, slander, and filthy language. Those things don't fit us anymore. They weigh us down. Now we put on compassion, kindness, humility, gentleness, patience, and love (Colossians 3:8, 12–14).

Paul realized that Christians couldn't do this all by themselves. In our own strength we can't always be patient on our job or with our family. We can't love others when they aren't loving toward us. We can't put aside feelings of anger and resentment when we feel they are warranted. We need God's power to put off the old self and put on the new.

Have you ever wished you could run into
a phone booth, change into a snazzy
costume, and come out with the extra power
you need to meet the demands of life?

As a reflection of popular culture, movies often reveal what people really want—and often what they really want is power. An awkward youth gets bitten by a radioactive spider and gains superhuman abilities. A mild-mannered newspaper reporter flies faster than a speeding bullet and leaps tall buildings in a single bound. Perhaps we're drawn to these kinds of fictional superheroes because we feel we need more power than we have. Have you ever wished you could run into a phone booth, change into a snazzy costume, and come out with the extra power you need to meet the demands of life?

GOD'S POWER

I have some great news: God has provided something much better for us. Romans 6:5 tells us that since we have been united with Christ in His death, we can be assured that the same power that raised

Him from the dead is available to us. His death and resurrection unite us with Him. You can run the race and win because you have divine power.

Ephesians 2:6 says that we have been raised with Christ. Most Christians consider this a past accomplishment. In Philippians 3:10, however, Paul says that one of his greatest aspirations was to actively know the power of Christ's resurrection. He wanted to grasp that power and use it to live free of sin's grip.

And he did.

In Ephesians 1:19, Paul wants us to know the kind of power that is available to all of us as God's kids. It is an incomparable power, a superhuman power, and an overcoming power.

An Incomparable Power

The apostle used three strong words to describe the spiritual force living inside us: "incomparably great power." Paul clearly states that this power is available to all believers. The power to live righteously comes from the Holy Spirit, a living force given only to believers. If you are a believer, the Holy Spirit is living in you, giving you the power to live a sanctified life (Romans 8:9–10).

A Superhuman Power

The second word for power in Ephesians 1:19 is "working," which comes from the same Greek word from which we get the English word *energy*. Not surprisingly, it means *energetic power*. Scripture uses this word to refer only to superhuman power. Simply by being born again through salvation in Christ, we have the Holy Spirit's "incomparably great power" residing in us, but our inheritance also includes the superhuman energetic power that gets us up and into action so that the Holy Spirit's power can be used.

That may sound like double-talk until you think about it. If your house is in need of a good vacuuming, you must have two things: the power of a working vacuum cleaner and the energy to physically get up and push it across the floor. One without the other is useless.

To live a sanctified life, you must have two things: the power to do what God has called you to do and the energy to get up and use the power you have.

Which is more difficult for you, believing that God has given you the power to serve Him, or actually getting up and doing what He has called you to do? Well, God supplies not only the power to serve Him, but also the energy to get up and do it.

An Overcoming Power

The third power Paul refers to is "the strength of His might." The Greek word for "strength" here means *power that overcomes resistance.* In Scripture, this term is used only of God, never of humans. The word used for "might" means *powerful ability.* So what Paul is saying is that God has the powerful ability to overcome any resistance. This is the same power He used to defeat death and the same power that placed Jesus Christ over "all rule and authority, power and dominion, and every title that can be given, not only in the present age but also in the one to come" (v. 21). This same power helps us overcome sin and live victorious lives.

Isn't our God amazing? He knows that we are weak in ourselves, so He supplies us with all the power we need. He gives the power supplied by the Spirit, the energy to get up and use that power, and the power to overcome the resistance we will face when we do. With all that power at our disposal, we don't have any excuse for not putting on righteousness.

The bad news is that when we become Christians, we don't just automatically stop sinning. We struggle with sin as long as we're on earth. The good news is that we can put on Christ and allow His power to flow through us and control us. In one sense, we have put on Christ once for all. In another sense, we must put on Christ daily.

Remember that holiness isn't about our own efforts; it's about yielding to the power of the Holy Spirit in our lives and allowing Him to work out His righteousness in and through us. So don't let the prospect of living a set-apart life overwhelm you. God is at work in you through the Holy Spirit to make it happen. All you have to do is surrender.

When most of us read phrases like "allowing Christ to live through us," we're tempted to ignore the implications these words have on our responsibility as Christians. In fact, if we are painfully honest, I suspect we would like to cut corners when it comes to living a sanctified life. I think of our church's front lawn. Congregants wanting to take a shortcut from one building to another have worn a new path there. The new trail leaves the sidewalk and cuts through the flowers and between the trees. Over the years, the path has become so obvious that everyone has started to use it.

Shortcuts may work to get from one building to another, but if we take them in the race Paul talks about, we'll never win the prize. When we ask ourselves what we can do to just get by as Christians— and then convince ourselves that it's okay because, after all, everyone's doing it—we aim not for the most, but for the least that we can be and do.

Personal holiness will never make God love us. He loves us because He is love and because His Son's blood covers us. Lifestyle sanctification will never take the place of a single drop of Christ's blood. When we stand before God, the only righteousness we will possess is Christ's, not our own. So if holiness can neither justify us nor make us acceptable, why should we bother? Because when we obey God in holiness, we bow at His feet, awaiting His Word.

WHERE ARE YOU NOW?

TAKE TIME FOR A GPS READING:

- What things are weighing me down and preventing me from running a good race?

- What am I holding on to that doesn't fit my new identity in Christ?

- When I've tried to live a holy life in my own power, what have been the results?

- Am I sure I'm even in the race?

❖ ❖ ❖

Lord, I want to win the prize and hear You say, "Well done!" I want to live a holy life and receive a crown of righteousness. Help me put off the things that weigh me down and put on the things that speed me on my way. I confess that I can't run the race in my own power and thank You that You have provided Yours. Thank You for coaching me and cheering me on.

❖ ❖ ❖

PART FOUR

A Still Attentiveness

The lamp of God had not yet gone out, and *Samuel was lying down* in the temple of the LORD.

—1 Samuel 3:3

❖

The fourth characteristic that we discover about Samuel is that he was lying down. He was *still*. All day long, Samuel had ministered to the Lord and done good things in the temple. Now his chores were done for the day, everything was quiet, and Eli was asleep. God was awake, however, and He had a message for Samuel. With his thoughts quiet and his emotions stilled, Samuel was positioned to hear God's voice.

Be Still

❖

Be still,

and know that I am God.

—Psalm 46:10

❖

My sister is a mother-of-the-earth kind of woman who likes to have her babies at home with a midwife. For those of you who also like to have your children that way, I want you to know I admire and respect you. But I think you're just as crazy as Chrystal is. I'm a firm believer in epidurals.

When I was pregnant with my first son, I spent the entire nine months praying about what I wanted my labor and delivery experience to be like. I had serious conversations with the Lord about what I did and didn't want to experience. I made it very clear. I even talked to Him about the whole epidural thing and how maybe I could do it without any medication. I believed it was possible until I actually went into labor.

I remember walking up and down the stark white hallways of Baylor Hospital in Dallas. My husband had me by the hand and I was in between contractions, so I was momentarily in my right mind. I looked over at my husband and said, "Honey, somebody has to go get me an epidural."

"Priscilla, don't you have faith?" he asked.

"Yes," I said. "I have great faith that the epidural is gonna work."

So they took me into the delivery room and had me sit on the edge of a bed. A sweet little nurse put her forehead against my forehead and wrapped her arms around me as the anesthesiologist stood behind me and explained what he was about to do. He told me to be still and then gave me the medication.

The One with the answer
is right here, but the problem is that
we won't sit still long enough for Him
to give us what we need.

It began to take effect immediately.

Hallelujah!

I was so grateful that I turned around, looked at him, and said, "I sure hope my baby looks just like you." I was serious.

"Priscilla," the anesthesiologist said, "you were a great patient because you were really still. Sometimes women are in so much pain that they keep shifting their weight from side to side. I have to stand there and wait until they quiet enough for me to give them the medication, because I can't give it to them while they're moving."

As I listened, it dawned on me. Maybe the Great Physician is waiting to give us something. The One with the answer is right here, but the problem is that we won't sit still long enough for Him to give us what we need.

First Samuel 3:3 tells us that Samuel was lying down when God spoke to him. All day long, Samuel had been busy ministering to the Lord and doing his temple chores. But even though he was doing good things, God didn't speak to him while he was busy. He knew that Samuel was too preoccupied to hear His message clearly. So He waited until the temple was quiet and Samuel was still.

Are you too busy to hear from God? Do you, like Samuel, need to cease your activity and hush the noise in your life so you can more clearly discern what your Father wants to say to you?

SIT DOWN AND BE STILL

August 2004 was a very frantic time in my life. Jerry Jr. was three weeks old and not sleeping through the night, which meant Momma wasn't sleeping through the night either. I was trying to prepare for a full schedule of speaking engagements even though I was running around after a two-year-old all day and not getting enough rest at night. My life was crazy, and it was a rough time for me.

Then one day—August 10th, to be exact—the Lord had a message for me. That morning I sat at my kitchen table before the sun had even come up and opened my Bible. It just so happened that the study for the day was the passage in John that describes the feeding of the five thousand. I'm sure you've heard the story.

A multitude of people had listened to Jesus teach all day long, and as evening approached, their stomachs began to growl. Jesus knew the people were hungry, and He had a discussion with the disciples about how to feed them. My Bible study started at Mark 6, verse 10: "Jesus said, 'Have the people sit down.'" With the very first words I laid my eyes on that day, Jesus said to me, "Priscilla, sit down. Be still."

That morning when God asked me to sit down, I had a couple

of questions for Him. The first was, "Why, Lord? I'm so busy. I have a to-do list a mile long. *Why* do You want me to sit down?" He told me to read the next verse, so I read verse 11: "Jesus then took the loaves, gave thanks, and distributed to those who were seated."

Don't miss that line: He distributed to those who were seated. Only those who were seated got food. When I asked Jesus why He wanted me to sit down, He said, "Priscilla, I want to fill you, but I can't fill you until you take your seat." God was asking me to cease my frantic activity and let go of my worry and frustration so He could minister to me.

Listen, do you want to be filled with the spiritual food God has for you? Then you'd better sit down, because He's only distributing fish and loaves to the people who are seated. We often miss out on His blessings because we just won't be still.

TOO BUSY SERVING

It was interesting to me that in this passage about the feeding of the five thousand, we have absolutely no record of the disciples eating. All it tells us is that they picked up the leftovers. The disciples were doing a good thing by serving, but they were so busy picking up the leftovers of everybody else's blessing that they missed out on being filled.

Now I don't mind picking up leftovers, but I also want to be one of the ones getting fed. This means that I must carve time out of my busy day to sit quietly in the presence of Jesus so He can speak to me. Are you missing out on what Jesus wants to say to you because you're so busy serving?

I think this might have been part of Martha's problem. The Lord and His disciples had dropped in for supper at the home of Martha, Lazarus, and Mary. Martha was running around madly trying to get food on the table. She expected her sister to help her, but Mary was just sitting at the Lord's feet, listening to Him. It was too much to take. So Martha went to Jesus and said, "Tell her to help me" (Luke 10:40).

"Martha, Martha," the Lord answered, "you are worried and up-set about many things, but only one thing is needed. Mary has cho-sen what is better, and it will not be taken away from her" (vv. 41–42).

Like so many of us, Martha was too busy serving to sit down, and so she was hungry and cranky. Mary, on the other hand, was sit-ting peacefully at the Lord's feet being filled with the Bread of Life.

Don't the *good* things often keep us too busy to sit still at Jesus' feet and receive the *best* of what He has for us? I think about my life and particularly how I use my home. Most often when I have people over, it's ministry related. We're busy doing those good things in our homes, but sometimes I've found that the Lord doesn't speak to me while I'm preparing for or in the midst of those good things. He doesn't speak when I'm "worried and upset about many things." He speaks to me when everybody's gone and the house is quiet. It's when my body, mind, and emotions are still that He ministers and speaks to me. This seemed to be the case with Samuel as well. It's not that God doesn't want us to serve—He does. It's just that we must find a balance between serving and spending time in His presence.

The next time we see Martha, she's still serving. That was her gift, after all. Mary is again sitting at the feet of Jesus—this time, she anoints His feet with perfume (John 12:1–3). Though no one seems to be helping Martha, she no longer seems distracted, and she isn't complaining.

My guess is that after Jesus' gentle reproach, Martha learned to take time out from serving to sit down and hear from her Lord. How-ever she rearranged her schedule, it worked, since her attitude was completely changed.

GREEN PASTURES

I had another question for the Lord on that August morning when He told me to sit down. "Well, Lord," I said, "You've told me why You want me to sit down, but *where* do You want me to sit?" He told me that He had provided a very special place for me.

John 6:10 says there was "plenty of grass in that place" where

Jesus fed the five thousand. Mark's account is more detailed. He says there was "much *green* grass in the place." Psalm 23:2 refers to a place like this with "green pastures." I love it that Jesus didn't take this multitude out to a desert wasteland with thorny, hard ground and tell them to have a seat. He took them to a lush place of green pastures.

When the Lord asks us to sit, He wants us to sit on green grass where we can rest in His love. What's the green grass? It's everything we know to be true of Him regardless of our circumstances—His Word, His promises, and what He's done for us.

When I was in graduate school at Dallas Theological Seminary, I was broke all the time. My parents lived twenty minutes away, but I was trying to prove I could live on my own, so I rented a room for eighty dollars a month in a house owned by Youth with a Mission. Like all seminary students, I always needed more money, often coming to the end of my money way before I came to the end of my month. I had to scrape up every coin I could to pay that eighty-dollar rent.

We are able to trust the Lord because we have a history with Him.

I knew the Lord had called me into ministry and wanted me in graduate school full-time, so I would pray, *Look, Lord, You have to pay the rent. I know I'm supposed to be in school. As far as I know, I'm doing what You called me to do. So I'm counting on You to come up with eighty dollars this month.*

I can't begin to tell you how many times I got to the end of the month without a dime in my pocket. But it would just happen to be the month of my birthday or a month when someone would call and ask me to do a Bible study and just happen to give me some money. God always provided some way to pay.

God's record of faithfulness meant there was green grass to sit on when God told my husband and me that we were to leave our jobs and jump into full-time women's ministry. We had two small children, a mortgage, car notes, insurance premiums, and other bills to pay, but you'd better believe that we could confidently obey God because He had proven Himself to us before. Even today, we are able to trust the Lord because we have a history with Him.

As Jesus got ready to feed the five thousand, He turned to the people and told them to sit on the green grass, and they confidently obeyed. Why? Because they knew what He had done. They had heard about the miracle at Cana where He had turned the water into wine. They had heard about how He had healed the royal official's son and the lame man beside the pool of Bethesda. So when this Jesus told them to sit down, they sat.

What's your history with God? When He asks you to sit down, remember what He's done for you in the past, because that's the lush place He has provided for you to sit.

God asks us to be still enough so we can hear what the Great Physician has to say to us and get the medication He wants to give us. I've discovered that God doesn't shout over my noise. He waits until I'm quiet. A calm and composed spirit is open to divine revelation and comfort.

Asking us to sit down is God's way of asking us to trust Him, to just relax and know that He'll take care of us. I pray that you'll yield to the Spirit's call and make a conscious effort to sit down and be still so that you, like Samuel, can hear God speak.

WHERE ARE YOU NOW?

TAKE TIME FOR A GPS READING:

- In what ways do I sense God telling me to be still so He can speak to me?

- Is my natural inclination to be busy and worried like Martha or more peaceful like Mary?

- What are some of the green pastures in my life?

- What conscious steps do I need to take to rearrange my schedule so that I can be still before God?

❖ ❖ ❖

Father, how grateful I am for the times You tell me to sit down and be still because You want to minister to me. I confess that at times I can't hear Your voice because I'm so busy. Please help the Martha in me learn to sit at Your feet, listening to You, as Mary did. Thank You for the green pastures You provide so I can rest comfortably and listen for Your voice.

❖ ❖ ❖

Strength in Surrender

❖

In repentance and rest is your salvation,

in quietness and trust is your strength.

—Isaiah 30:15

❖

My father was a lifeguard during college, and while I was growing up, he told me many stories about the times he had saved lives. On one occasion he saw a struggling man and swam out to meet him. However, he couldn't do anything to help because the man was so afraid that he was waving and kicking in an effort to save himself. Dad kept calling out to the man to be still, but the fearful young man wouldn't stop struggling. My father had no choice but to wait. He treaded water nearby until the drowning man got too tired to fight. As soon as he gave up and became still, my father swam in and did what he had intended to do all along: save one who might otherwise be lost.

God desires to speak to us, but we are often struggling so hard to solve our problems ourselves that we can't hear Him. Our panicky efforts keep us from hearing His calming voice, receiving His instructions, and allowing Him to do what He intended to do all along: save us when we might otherwise be lost.

Frantic physical activity wasn't the only thing keeping this man from being saved. So was his lack of confidence in the one who could save him. Humanity's fallen nature is like a two-year-old crying out, "I want to do it myself!" This impulse is so strong that we cling to it even when we are on the verge of perishing spiritually. Only God can save you, but you must cease your own efforts and rely completely on Him.

KNOW WHEN TO WAIT

When the Assyrian Empire was sweeping westward toward Canaan around 733 B.C., the Israelites tried to cement an alliance with their traditional enemy, Egypt. They thought that with the help of the Egyptian army, they would have the strength they needed to save themselves from the Assyrian onslaught.

The children of Israel were aligning themselves with the enemy God had delivered them from years earlier. But through the prophet Isaiah, God told the Israelites that they weren't going to find their strength in any alliance with the enemy. God said His people would find their strength in being still and trusting in Him. In other words, they needed to stop trying to fix the problem themselves. Time and again, God told His people the same thing.

When Pharaoh pursued the Israelites into the wilderness and penned them up between the desert and the sea, Moses told the terrified people, "Do not be afraid. Stand firm and you will see the deliverance the LORD will bring you today. . . . The LORD will fight for you; you need only to be still" (Exodus 14:13–14).

And when the Israelites were surrounded on all sides by a vast army, God told them they didn't need to fight (2 Chronicles 20). He told them to take up their positions, stand firm, and wait for the salvation of the Lord. When King Jehoshaphat saw the enemies approaching, he called for a national fast and sought the Lord. Instead of frantically seeking his own solution, he looked to God. A quick remembrance of these incidents in their history could have shown the Israelites what to do in their time of need.

> *We are called to take our place in the*
> *line of battle and stand firm.*

Though God continually offered the Israelites strength and salvation from their enemies if they would just be still, they usually did everything in their power to try to solve their problems on their own. Predictably, their efforts proved futile, and the outcome was almost always disastrous.

Are you currently in a situation you're trying to get out of on your own? Have you tried everything you know to do but yet find yourself in the same place? If so, the futility of your efforts may be the voice of God calling you to place your confidence in Him instead of in yourself. Satan knows we can find real peace and power in our lives when we turn to God and trust Him. That's why he desires nothing more than to keep us from being still and waiting on God.

Waiting doesn't call us to a passive life that requires no effort on our part. The decision to repent, be still, and trust is a conscious commitment that requires courage and diligence. We often want to take on a more aggressive role in fighting our personal battles, and it can be extremely difficult to respond to a challenge by waiting quietly before the Lord. But waiting is essential if we want the victory. One of the most important people on the battlefield was the watchman who sat still for days on end with his eyes peeled for approaching enemies. We are called to take our place in the line of battle and stand firm.

While you're holding down your spot on the battle line, don't think that Satan won't attack you, because he will. Peter tells us that our "enemy the devil prowls around like a roaring lion looking for someone to devour" (1 Peter 5:8). There will be skirmishes to fight while we're waiting for God's salvation, and the place Satan is most likely to attack us is on the battlefield of our mind.

THE BATTLE IN OUR MINDS

I know a young woman who struggled with an eating disorder for more than a decade. She said that she knew Satan used her mind to keep her in bondage by continually filling it with destructive thoughts, from doubt to worry to self-condemnation. These thoughts kept her from recognizing God's love and hearing His voice. You can probably think of people like my friend. You yourself may be struggling with an overwhelming addiction or compulsion. We know a battle is raging when we can't sleep, eat, or think straight because of the tug-of-war going on in our heads.

We have to recognize that our minds are battlefields, not theme parks. Our thoughts are one of the hardest areas for us to control, yet they are often the easiest for Satan to use against us. Our imaginations, thoughts, and even our dreams can fuel every kind of negative thought from lust to guilt to revenge, filling our mind with images that can pull us away from the Lord, His voice, and His plan for our lives. The Enemy's goal is to keep our minds so occupied that we don't hear God's voice.

The apostle Paul understood that believers don't wage war as the world does. Our Enemy is a spiritual being who fights a spiritual war against us. Paul tells us that Satan has built two fortresses to prevent people from getting close to God and hearing from Him. He calls these strongholds "imaginations" and "every high thing that is exalted against the knowledge of God" (2 Corinthians 10:5 ASV).

The warfare for our minds requires spiritual weapons with divine power to scale the ramparts of Satan's fortresses and demolish them. Seminars, counseling, and discussions can be wonderful tools, but in themselves they aren't adequate to scale the ramparts of Satan's fortresses and demolish them.

In Ephesians 6, Paul lists our weapons and tells us to "put on the full armor of God" (v. 11). The piece of spiritual armor that protects our thought life is the helmet of salvation. Having our heads covered with it keeps us safe and helps us stand firm and fight with confidence as we demolish strongholds.

When I face a challenge, Satan says to me, "You know you're a failure. You've faced this before, and you've failed before. God is disappointed in you. You can't do anything right." Then I read God's Word, and it assures me that all my sin has been covered by Christ's blood. It tells me Christ loves me and that Satan is the crown prince of liars.

Boom! There goes another stronghold.

> *As legitimate as emotions are,*
> *our feelings should never have*
> *the final say in our lives.*

The Word of God is the sword of the Spirit (v. 17), and it enables us to "take captive every thought to make it obedient to Christ" (2 Corinthians 10:5). When the Holy Spirit supernaturally applies the Word of God to our life, we can begin to take our thoughts captive. When I purposefully fill my mind with the Word of God, particularly before retiring for the night, my thoughts focus not on my day but on what I've just read. The very power of God through the living words of Scripture combats the strongholds that take up residence in my mind.

Every time inappropriate thoughts infiltrate your mind, quickly jab those thoughts with the sword of the Word. Dwell on the validity of Scripture to combat the dishonest and unreliable messages you receive from the Devil and the world. If we want God to speak to us, we must keep our minds free of thoughts that stand in the way.

I'm pleased to tell you that my friend who struggled with an eating disorder is winning the war against it. She told me that to combat the Enemy of her soul she purposely fills her mind with the Word of God. As she takes her thoughts captive, she is also able to be still in her emotions. Her fear of gaining weight no longer has the final say in her life.

HALT YOUR RUNAWAY FEELINGS

If challenges and hard times make you fearful, sad, or angry, you're certainly not alone. Emotions are not wrong. Scripture doesn't say that we shouldn't feel. In fact, God Himself exhibits many emotions ranging from joy to anger. Jesus felt a sadness that caused Him to weep, and though He was sinless, He experienced anger. The problem is that many of us allow our feelings to dictate our actions and justify our decisions.

As legitimate as emotions are, our feelings should never have the final say in our lives. Emotions are fickle and change at a moment's notice. A good movie can have most of us crying one moment and laughing the next. Paul clearly warns that allowing our emotions to gain control of our actions gives Satan an opportunity to work in our lives: "Be angry, and yet do not sin; do not let the sun go down on your anger, and do not give the devil an opportunity" (Ephesians 4:26–27 NASB).

When Jackson was three months old, we moved him from the bassinet in our room to his nursery upstairs. How far away that nursery seemed during that first month of separation! I couldn't sleep. My imagination conjured up all kinds of improbable scenarios, like the neighbor's cat getting in the house and smothering Jackson in his crib or a tornado ripping off the roof above the nursery. Fear consumed me and left me wide-awake.

My fear exposed the gap between what I felt and what I said I believed. What it came down to was this: Did I or did I not believe that God was in full control? If I did, I had a decision to make. Would I allow fear to control my actions by stealing my sleep or making me sleep in the nursery? Or would I let go of my fears and give them to God?

How about you? You may not confess to fears as unrealistic as mine, or as a mother you may have felt exactly the same. Either way, you probably know about what comes next—our fears begin to snowball. Emotions don't like being alone, and they often invite their friends in for a sledding party. When Satan gets to our emotions, they begin to snowball and run downhill, getting bigger and dirtier as they roll.

Remembering God's promises helps us stop our runaway emotions. Moses didn't just tell the Israelites to stop being afraid; he also gave them a reason to relinquish their fears. He said, "The LORD will fight for you." Time and time again God tells His people that they need not fear because He Himself will act on their behalf:

- "The word of the LORD came to Abram in a vision: 'Do not be afraid, Abram. I am your shield, your very great reward.'" (Genesis 15:1)
- "Do not be afraid or terrified because of them, for the LORD your God goes with you; he will never leave you nor forsake you." (Deuteronomy 31:6)
- "Do not be afraid or discouraged, for the LORD God, my God, is with you." (1 Chronicles 28:20)
- "I am the LORD, your God, who takes hold of your right hand and says to you, 'Do not fear; I will help you.'" (Isaiah 41:13)

God's promises can act as the catalyst we need to relinquish emotions that threaten to consume us.

John 3:16 clearly states that God sent His Son to die for those who needed saving, but that salvation only comes to those who *believe in Him*. Our walk with Christ began when we removed the confidence we had in our abilities to save ourselves, and we decided to trust Him instead. Just as salvation can come only when we transfer our confidence from ourselves to Jesus, our ability to live victorious Christian lives comes only as we place that same confidence in Christ each day.

Whether in business or personal matters, it can be so easy to trust in ourselves but so difficult to face our weaknesses, admit our fears, and ask God for the help we need.

Yet we must recognize our limitations, because only Christ can take care of our problems. When we do that, God promises that "the peace of God, which transcends all understanding, will guard your hearts and your minds in Christ Jesus" (Philippians 4:7).

When David was living on the run because King Saul was trying to kill him, I'm sure there must have been many nights when fear threatened to rob him of his sleep. Yet David could still say, "I will lie down and sleep in peace, for you alone, O LORD, make me dwell in safety" (Psalm 4:8).

David's complete confidence in the Lord put him in the perfect position to hear from God, for "when sound sleep falls on men, while they slumber in their beds, then He opens the ears of men, and seals their instruction" (Job 33:15–16 NASB).

WHERE ARE YOU NOW?

❖

TAKE TIME FOR A GPS READING:

- Do I tend to handle my problems more as the Israelites did in Isaiah's day, or as they did in Jehoshaphat's day?

- How do I calm my mind when I feel it filling with negative thoughts?

- Can I think of times when I have let my emotions have the final say in my decisions?

- How confident am I that the Lord will act on my behalf if I am still and wait on Him?

❖ ❖ ❖

*Lord, I have trusted You for my eternal salvation, and I
thank You for sending Your Son to die for me. Now I want
to learn to trust You to save me day by day. I confess that I
need Your strength to solve my problems, to keep my
thoughts focused on Your truths, and to keep my emotions
from ruling my actions. But most of all, Father God,
I want to learn to quiet my thoughts and emotions
so I can be still in Your presence.*

❖ ❖ ❖

A Mature
Peace

❖

My soul finds rest in God alone.

—Psalm 62:1

❖

eaning Jackson after I'd nursed him for a year was difficult for both of us. I knew it was time for him to drink milk from a cup, but I hated to turn him down when he wanted to nurse. During the two days it took to wean him, he was a mess. He was restless, anxious, and cried continuously. Since he couldn't have what he had previously depended on and still desired, he thought his world had turned upside down.

My job during this period was to soothe and quiet him. He needed to be consoled. I rocked him, kept him occupied, and did my best to make sure he understood that all would be well. And every time he wanted to nurse, I offered him a cup of warm milk. Later, Jackson no longer looked to me to nurse him. When he wanted milk, he knew it came from the refrigerator. His soul was calm, and he rested in his new situation.

Just as we can't remain infants physically, God doesn't intend for us to remain spiritual babies. In fact, He wants us to wean ourselves from everything that keeps us from depending on Him so that we can grow spiritually. Once our souls are weaned, they find their rest in Him.

First Samuel 3:15 says that after God spoke to him, "Samuel lay down until morning and then opened the doors of the house of the LORD." How do you think Samuel slept after God told him that Eli's family was going to be cut off from the priesthood and his two sons were about to die? If it had been me, I think I would have been pacing the floor of the temple trying to figure out what I was going to do the next day.

But the Bible says that Samuel "lay down until morning." I think Samuel could sleep well and go confidently about his business the next morning because his life was aligned with God's plans for him. Samuel had weaned himself from depending on his own efforts, and his soul was still and quiet. He was resting in peace, depending upon God to show Himself strong in him.

A QUIETED SOUL

As David prepared to ascend the throne of Israel, he confessed his inadequacy: "My heart is not proud, O LORD, my eyes are not haughty; I do not concern myself with great matters or things too wonderful for me" (Psalm 131:1). The powerful man who would soon be king didn't take credit for the blessings in his life; instead, he made himself more dependent upon God by weaning himself from his own talents and ambitions and trusting in the Lord as a child trusts a loving parent.

To have an intimate relationship with the Father, all believers must eventually come to the point where they courageously tear themselves away from things that keep them from depending completely upon God. However, none of us will wean ourselves from our dependence on worldly things without discipline and discomfort. By the power of the Holy Spirit, we have to purposefully and oftentimes painfully deny ourselves. When we begin the weaning process, we may feel uneasy, fretful, and uncomfortable. But with practice, it becomes easier to turn to God for comfort and spiritual nourishment.

> *If we continue to allow God to fill us,*
> *sooner or later we'll find that*
> *nothing else will satisfy.*

I'm sure that at times David's soul cried out for the things he had once depended on. He said: "I have stilled and quieted my soul; like a weaned child with its mother" (v. 2). When a mother weans an infant, she must soothe the child, just as I did with Jackson. But as children grow, they learn to soothe themselves. So it was with David. He deliberately calmed himself so that, like a weaned child who has learned to trust his mother, he could walk trustingly beside God the Father.

When David's heart was restless during the process, he wrote: "Why are you downcast, O my soul? Why so disturbed within me? Put your hope in God, for I will yet praise him, my Savior and my God" (Psalm 42:5). Just as a cup of warm milk calmed Jackson's anxiety, David's hope in God consoled and comforted his anxious soul.

Jeremiah uses a graphic image to describe the practice of depending on anything other than God to meet our needs. He says the Israelites have forsaken "the spring of living water, and have dug their own cisterns, broken cisterns that cannot hold water" (Jeremiah 2:13). Broken cisterns don't hold water, so they can't satisfy.

- Money is a broken cistern.
- Success is a broken cistern.
- Beauty is a broken cistern.
- Ego is a broken cistern.

What is your broken cistern? If we seek fulfillment in the things of the world after a season of depending on God, we will discover that they don't satisfy us the way they once did. And if we continue to allow God to fill us, sooner or later we'll find that nothing else will satisfy.

We depend on what we know. When we have a trust relationship with other people, we gladly depend on them. Likewise, when we place our trust in God, we naturally depend on Him. The more you trust your concerns to the Lord and see Him working in your life, the more willing you will be to depend on Him in the future. Hallelujah, God never disappoints!

JOINED AT THE HIP

As a speaker and Bible teacher, I talk to thousands of women every year. Over time I've learned that I have to be careful not to rely on my communication skills or familiarity with the message. When I rely on those instead of the power of the Holy Spirit, the message lacks the power and anointing that causes the message to actually change lives. But when I confess my inadequacy, let go of my self-reliance, and depend completely on the Lord, He touches hearts and changes lives in ways I never could.

Self-reliance and ambition are joined at the hip. I used to proudly define myself as an ambitious person. Then the Lord revealed to me the sinful nature of ambition apart from dependence upon Him. We must not allow our ambitions to drown out the sound of God's voice.

Our ambitions often reveal a deeper desire for status, fame, or power. Most of what we strive for finds its root in one of those three areas. Paul calls relying on ourselves to fill these desires "confidence in the flesh" (Philippians 3:3–4). If anyone ever had the right to have confidence in himself, it was the apostle Paul. Have you ever read his résumé? If not, you can find it in verse 5.

- He was circumcised on the eighth day. (He was a keeper of God's Law from the start.)
- He was from the nation of Israel and the tribe of Benjamin. (He was from the right culture.)
- He was a Hebrew of Hebrews. (He was socially acceptable.)
- He was a Pharisee. (He was religiously upstanding.)

We might think that Paul had a résumé to die for. Paul, however, considered it a résumé to die *to*, for it represented the legalistic righteousness that made him ambitious to persecute the church of Jesus Christ. Worldly ambition is the desire to find fulfillment in the things that please us instead of the things that please God. Like Paul, we should say, "Whatever was to my profit I now consider loss for the sake of Christ" (v. 7).

Before I understood God's calling on my life, I wanted to be a Christian singer. I prepared myself by rehearsing and singing at every opportunity. I surrounded myself with key people in the industry and successful Christian artists and sought advice on what steps to take and when to take them. Nothing happened. Discouraged, I became worried as door after door closed in my face.

Instead of accepting the sound of slamming doors as a sign that God wanted me to move in a different direction, I allowed my ambition to make me self-reliant. I began trying to kick down the doors of the music industry on my own. My desire to sing controlled me. I made phone calls, sent tapes, and tried to create opportunities to sing. I did everything I could to make things happen. But nothing did, because God had other plans for me.

God gives us the freedom to prepare, plan, and position ourselves to achieve our goals. Ultimately, however, we must let go of our self-sufficiency, relaxing in the knowledge that God is sovereign and that His design and purposes for our lives are better than our own.

The sound of opening and closing doors is one way we hear from God. But too often we don't hear His voice clearly because our ambitions get in the way. We don't really want to hear from God because we're afraid He might ask us to do something that goes against our own plans. When we calm our souls and make it our ambition to rely completely upon Him for the path we take in life, we will inevitably hear His voice more clearly.

Peace Rules

Another way God speaks to us is through peace, or the lack thereof. Peace is a crucial component in hearing God's voice and deciphering His will. Paul says, "Let the peace of Christ rule in your hearts . . . and be thankful" (Colossians 3:15 NASB). I'm learning to recognize the presence or absence of the peace of Christ.

When we get off track,
we experience symptoms of dis-ease—
dissatisfaction, guilt, and anxiety.

Recently, my husband and I were at odds about a particular situation, so I did what I thought was appropriate: I kept bringing it up! I did it in a way that seemed very loving to me. I put a smile on my face, waited until the appropriate time, and made sure I was not nagging. (At least it didn't sound like nagging to me.)

Outwardly, I was confident about my decision to keep discussing the situation, but deep down inside I wasn't at peace. Every time I decided to bring up the issue, I felt the Ruler of my heart throw up a warning flag, yet ahead I went. I spoke in what sounded to me like a peaceful tone, but I was blatantly ignoring the lack of peace in my heart. As a result, both my peace and my marriage suffered.

As Christians we have a built-in meter to gauge our behavior. The

Holy Spirit works in us, continually urging us to check our actions against what we know is right. When we get off track, we experience symptoms of *dis-ease*—dissatisfaction, guilt, and anxiety. But when our lives align with God's plans, we find peace.

Peace is a gift that accompanies salvation. As believers, we are not on a search for peace: it's already available to us. Peace results from God's presence in our lives. It calms, reassures, and comforts. Peace brings rest, tranquility, and assurance. When we experience the lack of quiet rest, we need to ask if our hearts may be sensing the absence of God's presence or approval. Never take lightly decisions or plans that leave your heart in turmoil. When you feel a tug-of-war ensuing in your heart, pay close attention. Peace or a lack of it can settle a debate or argument for you and lead you to make correct decisions.

In high school I dated a football player, and one afternoon he invited me to his house. My parents had instructed me never to go to a boy's home unchaperoned. I knew this boy's parents weren't home, but I tried to ignore the fact. I'll never forget the war that ensued in my heart as we prepared to go. A lack of peace immediately flooded my heart. The Holy Spirit was warning me, but I shrugged off the warning and went anyway.

Within an hour I was face-to-face with the reason for the Ruler's warning. This young man, whom I had known throughout school, became a different person. His boyish charm turned to aggression, leaving me in an awful position. While the Lord spared me from what could have been a horrible outcome, I hurt for the thousands of women who haven't been as fortunate.

When we ignore the agitation in our heart, we plunge ourselves into a period of turmoil. King David sinned greatly by committing adultery with Bathsheba and then arranging a cover-up by sending her husband to the front line of battle where he would be killed. For a year, David lived with his unconfessed sin. Then, after the prophet Nathan confronted him, David confessed. He wrote a psalm to tell us what that time was like:

When I refused to confess my sin,
I was weak and miserable,
and I groaned all day long.
Day and night your hand of discipline was heavy on me.
My strength evaporated like water in the summer heat.
Finally, I confessed all my sins to you
and stopped trying to hide them.
I said to myself, "I will confess my rebellion to the Lord."
And you forgave me! All my guilt is gone. (Psalm 32:3–5 NLT)

Although David's disquieted soul finally confessed his sin, it is possible to have peace when we're outside the will of God. We can experience the false peace of a dull conscience. Jesus slept soundly in a boat on a stormy sea (Luke 8:23–24). Jonah did the same (Jonah 1:5). Jesus was the incarnate God; Jonah was running from God. Yes, it is possible to ignore the voice of God and still get a good night's sleep.

The Bible gives us several practical ways to discern God's will and distinguish between true and false peace. These red flags can help you determine if you're outside God's will even when you sleep soundly at night. Let's take a quick look at them.

Red Flag #1: Are you running away? After receiving difficult instructions from God, Jonah's first action was to run away (Jonah 1:3). He tried to create as much distance as he could between himself and God.

Red Flag #2: Are you compensating? You can tell something is wrong internally if you're trying to fill the void with external things. Most of us could name a time when we've tried to fill an inner void with some substance or behavior.

Red Flag #3: Are you thankful? Did you notice the last words of Colossians 3:15? Not only are we to allow Christ's peace to rule in our hearts, but we are also to "be thankful." Thanksgiving is always connected to the outpouring of God's peace.

God gives us peace as a means to discover where He is leading us. When you and I walk in God's will, peace will rule our hearts regardless of our circumstances. In making decisions that glorify God, we must constantly ask, "Am I experiencing God's peace regarding this decision?"

God's presence and the peace He provides go hand in hand. Even when He disciplines us, the end result is restored peace. By deliberately quieting his soul, calming his ambition, and confessing his sins, David found himself at rest and in a position to hear from God.

WHERE ARE YOU NOW?

❖

TAKE TIME FOR A GPS READING:

- In what way do I need to wean myself from worldly things to draw closer to God?

- Have I ever persisted in my plans even when I heard the sound of slamming doors? What was the result?

- How might self-sufficiency and ambition be hurting my ability to hear from God?

- How does my dis-ease manifest itself when I have unconfessed sin in my life?

❖❖❖

Lord, forgive me for the times I have depended on other things and people when I should have placed my trust in You. I confess my self-sufficiency and put You back into first place in my life. Help me through the rough stages as I quiet my soul. Still my ambitious heart and show me clearly Your will for me by closing the wrong doors and giving me Your peace. I'm excited about what You will reveal to me about Yourself as I give You an opportunity to show Yourself strong in me.

❖❖❖

PART FIVE

A Sold-Out Hunger

Samuel was lying down in the temple of the LORD,
where the ark of God was.

—1 Samuel 3:3

❖

The fifth thing we discover about Samuel is that he was

lying down right outside the *Holy of Holies* when he heard

God's voice. The Holy of Holies was where God dwelt,

but a curtain stood between it and Samuel. Because Samuel

had a sold-out hunger for God, he snuggled up right

next to the veil to get as close to Him as he possibly could.

Within Reach

❖

*Let us then approach the throne of grace
with confidence, so that we may receive mercy
and find grace to help us in our time of need.*

—Hebrews 4:16

❖

One day while I was flipping through channels I came across a program on MTV called *Total Request Live*. A celebrity was on the program, and an interviewer was asking her a lot of questions. There was a small studio audience, but most of the fans were down on the streets of New York watching through a wall of windows. I'll bet the fans on the street wished they were in the studio, but they didn't have access. All they could do was watch that celebrity from afar.

That must have been how Samuel felt. Samuel was hungry to be in the presence of God, but there was a barrier between them. The temple veil was a curtain that separated the Holy of Holies from the Holy Place where Samuel slept. Only the high priest could go beyond the veil and only on the Day of Atonement. Not even *he* could enter the Holy of Holies whenever he wanted. No matter how close Samuel wanted to be to God, going beyond the veil would have meant certain death. But Samuel knew that God was there, so the night God spoke to him, he was sleeping as close as he could get to the Holy of Holies.

Christ's death on the cross removed the barrier between us and the Holy of Holies. The moment Christ died, the curtain of the temple was torn in two (Matthew 27:51; Mark 15:38; Luke 23:45). What this means for us is that there is no longer anything standing between God and us. Unlike Samuel, we have direct access to the presence of the biggest Celebrity in the universe.

I'm not just talking about God's *omnipresence*. Whether we like it or not, we all experience the fact that God is present everywhere all at the same time, because that's just a part of who God is. I'm talking about His *manifest presence*. This is His obvious, palpable presence.

When you're experiencing God's manifest presence, you can see His handiwork in your life. And when you look back over your history, you can see the footprints of where He has been. You can see evidence of His power at work around you and hear His voice clearly as He guides you. This is what is available to you and me right now.

We don't have Samuel's problem, but we do need Samuel's passion. We need to be hungry to approach God's throne of grace and receive "mercy and . . . grace to help us in our time of need" (Hebrews 4:16).

REACH OUT AND TOUCH HIM

In 2004, President Bush visited our church in Dallas. I cannot begin to tell you the drama involved when the president of the United States visits your church. Months beforehand, the Secret Service sent agents to check things out and make sure everything was secure. The day of the event, the helicopters hovered in the sky and SWAT teams crouched on the rooftop. Tentlike material was draped over every entrance so that no one could see in and no one could see out. Only certain people had access to the president, and on that day our family were to be among them. We were told beforehand that they needed our fingerprints so they could do background checks. My little boy was six months old at the time, and they checked him out too.

As I saw all that went into protecting the president and all the precautions that were taken to keep him away from direct contact with anyone, I thought that even though we don't have access to the president of the United States, we do have access to the Ruler of the universe. There are no barricades or background checks. There are no SWAT teams on the roof and no helicopters in the sky. Nothing stands between Him and us. God doesn't just stand afar and dangle Himself like a carrot to tease us. He gets close enough so we can reach out and touch Him.

Can you believe that someone as holy as God, someone who knows all the stuff in our closet and what we're thinking every moment, still makes Himself accessible to us? In Psalm 8:3–4, David says, "When I consider your heavens, the work of your fingers, the moon and the stars, which you have set in place, what is man that you are mindful of him, the son of man that you care for him?" David couldn't believe it. Can you? I stand in awe that a God as great as that would let us touch Him. But He does.

Luke tells many stories of how Jesus made Himself accessible to people who passionately pursued Him. Consider the story in Luke 8 about the woman who had been bleeding for twelve years. No physician could help her. She was undoubtedly anemic and tired. Yet she managed to push her way through a crowd of people so she could get close to Jesus. She may have wanted to speak to Him and explain her situation, but by the time she got through that crowd, it took all the energy she had left just to fall to her knees and touch the hem of His garment as He walked by.

Jesus already had something else on His to-do list. A man had approached the Lord to ask Him to heal his critically ill daughter, and Jesus was making His way through the crowd to the girl's bedside. Yet when the desperate woman reached out and touched Him, He stopped. Jesus stopped for that woman and asked, "Who touched me?" (v. 45).

Peter tried to explain that no one had deliberately touched Jesus; it was just the crowd jostling Him.

But as usual the Lord knew better than Peter. "'Someone touched me,'" He said. "'I know that power has gone out from me'" (v. 46).

Trembling, the woman fell at Jesus' feet and told Him why she had touched Him and what the result had been. She had been instantly healed.

"Daughter," Jesus said, "your faith has healed you. Go in peace" (v. 48).

Sister, when you are desperate to meet Jesus, reach out and touch Him. He will stop and respond.

NEEDING HIS LEADING

The symbol of God's presence with the Israelites was the ark of the covenant. A rather small wooden box covered with gold, the ark housed the Israelites' holy objects—the Ten Commandments, a sample of manna, and Aaron's staff. God made His presence known to Israel by dwelling there.

The ark of the covenant is currently lost to history, but God's presence is not.

The Israelites often carried the ark into battle with them because it meant that God was right there with them, fighting for them. When God told Joshua to conquer Jericho, He ordered the Israelites to take the ark into battle as the sign of His presence. Surrounded by armed guards, seven priests were to carry the ark of the covenant around the city once a day for six days. That was all they were to do. On the seventh day they were to carry the ark around the city seven times and then give a great shout.

The Israelites obeyed all of God's instructions, and the rest is history. As the song says, "the walls came a-tumblin' down." Many years later, the Israelites took the ark into another battle. But that time they did it without orders from God, and the outcome was far different.

First Samuel 4:1–7 tells the story of a great defeat the Philistines handed the Hebrews. The disaster was so great that the Israelites sent men to bring the ark of the covenant into their camp. This was a sinful act for two reasons: First, they did it without asking God for instructions; second, they were treating the ark as if it were some sort of good luck charm. Nevertheless, Eli's sons, the priests Hophni and Phineas, accompanied the ark to the Israelites' camp.

When the ark arrived, the Israelites gave a great cheer, but the Philistines trembled. "A god has come into the camp," they said. "We're in trouble!" (v. 7). They understood as well as the Hebrews did that God's presence equals God's power.

The story doesn't end there, however. Despite the fact that the ark was in the Israelites' camp, God had withdrawn His presence. Because of their sin, He was not fighting for His people this time. So when the Philistines decided to fight, they not only defeated the Israelites again, but also captured the ark of the covenant and killed Hophni and Phineas. When Eli heard that his sons had been killed, he fell backward out of his chair, broke his neck, and died. God had fulfilled the prophecy He had entrusted to Samuel.

Though the Spirit dwells in us, it is up
to us to tap into the power He provides.

The ark of the covenant is currently lost to history, but God's presence is not. God now manifests His awesome presence through the power of the Holy Spirit. This is greatly to our advantage because now we don't need to see a wooden box to experience the power of the manifest presence of God. Wherever we go, His presence goes too because He is with us.

When you and I accepted Christ, God gave us the Holy Spirit as a birthday gift. The moment we became believers in Christ, we received all of the Holy Spirit we are ever going to receive. Though we can't physically see the Spirit, the effects of His presence are visible:

- He gives us everything we need to live godly lives (2 Peter 1:3).
- He convicts us of our sin (John 16:8).
- He teaches us what Jesus said (John 14:26).
- He guides us into all truth (John 16:13).

The word *power* summarizes what the Holy Spirit brings to believers (Acts 1:8). The Spirit is always working as an invisible power source inside us. But though the Spirit dwells in us, it is up to us to tap into the power He provides.

> *Going into the Holy of Holies*
> *would have cost Samuel his life.*
> *Not going in will cost us ours.*

In Ephesians 5:14–18, Paul refers to Christians who are spiritually asleep. We can choose to live without a passion for spiritual things and sleepwalk through life without experiencing the Spirit's power and leading. Hungry people do whatever is necessary to be filled, and when we show God that we are spiritually hungry, He responds.

CHANGED

When something fills us, it controls us. It changes the way we think and act and gives us the power to do things we might not normally have the power to do. Ephesians 5:18 contrasts being filled with the Spirit with drunkenness. Think about how too much alcohol changes a person's personality. When people are drunk, they do things they wouldn't normally do. Quiet, polite people can become loud and obnoxious. Shy people can put a lamp shade on their head, get up on a table, and dance. Being controlled by the presence and power of the Holy Spirit will also show in our actions. He enables us to live and act as we would not or could not on our own.

Just as God gave Moses the power to continue his journey to the Promised Land, He has given each of us the power to live a victorious Christian life. This means we ought to see a change when we're under the influence of His power. In Ephesians 5, Paul illustrates the change that being filled with the Spirit makes. I've broken verses 19–21 into phrases so you can't miss them:

- speaking to one another in psalms and hymns and spiritual songs
- singing and making music to the Lord
- always giving thanks for all things in the name of Jesus Christ
- being subject to one another in the fear of Christ

Those are pretty major changes for most of us. I know I wouldn't naturally act in those ways apart from the power of the Spirit. When the Spirit controls us, we become able to do what we could not do in and of ourselves.

Going into the Holy of Holies would have cost Samuel his life. Not going in will cost us ours. It's in God's presence that we tap into His life-giving power. Through the shed blood of God's Son, we now have access to God. All it takes is what Samuel had—a sold-out hunger for Him.

On the night Samuel heard God's voice, he didn't choose to sleep close to the chambers of Eli; he chose to sleep close to the chambers of his God. His passion was clearly to get close to God and God alone. If you're trying to snuggle up to your Bible study teacher, your pastor, or that author whose books you love to read, your priorities are mixed-up. Your consuming passion should be to get close to God, not them.

What's keeping you from experiencing God's manifest presence? Is your schedule overbooked? Is your job beating you down? Don't let that stand in your way. Is your marriage going through a rough patch? Are your children difficult to deal with right now? Don't let that hinder you.

God is accessible. Reach out and touch Him. He will stop and speak to you.

WHERE ARE YOU NOW?

❖

TAKE TIME FOR A GPS READING:

• What barriers have I erected between the Holy of Holies and me?

• Do I ever think of my relationship with God as somewhat of a good luck charm?

• How has being indwelt by the Holy Spirit changed my behavior?

• Am I more passionate about getting close to teachers of the Bible than I am to the God of the Bible?

❖ ❖ ❖

Father God, how grateful I am that You have given me access to You and that I can come boldly into Your throne room where I find mercy and grace and Your life-giving power. Lord Jesus, thank You for dying for me and tearing down the veil. I'm hungry for You, and only You can satisfy. Lord, right now I reach out and touch You and ask You to fill me, control me, and change me.

❖ ❖ ❖

FOURTEEN

Hungry for His Presence

❖

Blessed are you who hunger now,

for you will be satisfied.

—Luke 6:21

❖

I found out later that his name was Ron. But the day I met him he was just a guy replacing some countertops in our kitchen. When he saw my Bible on the kitchen table, he started to talk.

"Before I met Christ," he said, "I was addicted to sex, drugs, and alcohol. I even thought about leaving my family in my effort to fill my gnawing hunger. Everything I tried left me empty, but I kept looking. Then one day God showed up."

One morning a bad hangover kept Ron from being able to recall the events of the previous night. Something inside him snapped. As his tears flowed, a verse his wife had quoted many times echoed inside his head: "Call to me and I will answer you and tell you great and unsearchable things you do not know" (Jeremiah 33:3).

"God, if You are there and can hear me, I'm desperate," Ron cried.

Jesus met him there, and for the first time in Ron's life the void in his heart was filled. He never had another drink and never touched another drug, and he has been faithful to his wife and children since that day.

God meets with those who are hungry for His presence. He meets them where they are, satisfies their hunger, and changes their lives forever.

DESPERATE TO MEET JESUS

Luke 19 says that a man named Zacchaeus wanted to see Jesus as He passed through Jericho, but he was so short that he couldn't see over the heads of the crowd. Desperate to see the Master, he climbed a tree. When Jesus passed under the tree, He looked up and said, "Zacchaeus, come down immediately. I must stay at your house today" (v. 5).

Luke says that Zacchaeus immediately climbed down from the tree and welcomed the Lord. The crowd, however, wasn't so pleased. Zacchaeus, you see, was short *of* stature as well as *in* stature. He was a wealthy tax collector, which in the minds of those present meant he was a great sinner. But whom did Jesus have dinner with that night? Not the Pharisees in the crowd. He had dinner with Zacchaeus, the tax collector who was desperate enough to climb a tree in order to get in Jesus' presence. As a result of his passion to see Jesus, Zacchaeus achieved an intimacy with the Messiah that most of the crowd would never experience.

Zacchaeus's encounter with Jesus immediately changed his life. He promised to give half his possessions to the poor and to pay back four times the amount of anything he had cheated people out of.

"Today salvation has come to this house," Jesus said. "For the Son of Man came to seek and to save what was lost" (vv. 9–10).

Luke tells us about another outcast who was literally desperate to see Jesus. His name was Bartimaeus, and he was blind. Bartimaeus was on the roadside begging when he heard a crowd approaching. When he asked the people around him what was happening, they told him that Jesus was passing by. "Jesus, Son of David," the blind beggar called out, "have mercy on me!" (Luke 18:39).

Bartimaeus had heard about all the incredible things Jesus had been teaching and all the miracles the Master had been working on behalf of people who needed healing. He had heard about Jesus from afar, but I'll bet he never thought this Jesus would come his way. He was just a beggar. I'm sure Bartimaeus thought that people like him didn't stand a chance of experiencing the miracle of the power and presence of the Messiah.

But, suddenly, there Jesus was:

> Jesus stopped and ordered the man to be brought to him. When he came near, Jesus asked him, "What do you want me to do for you?"
>
> "Lord, I want to see," he replied.
>
> Jesus said to him, "Receive your sight; your faith has healed you." Immediately he received his sight and followed Jesus, praising God. (Luke 18:40–43)

Jesus was no longer far-off. He was standing right in front of Bartimaeus asking what He could do for him. Jesus made Himself available to a desperate man, and it changed that beggar's life forever.

*Your friends will know
what's most important to you
by what you talk about.*

For much of my Christian life, I felt like Bartimaeus must have. I'd heard about the great things Jesus had done for others and about how they clearly heard God's voice, but I hadn't experienced His manifest presence myself—and I thought I never would.

Praise God that experiencing His presence and hearing His voice is not just for the spiritual elite. It's for housewives and single women and blue-collar women and recovering women. It's for those of us who are overlooked and underappreciated. The King of Kings and Lord of Lords makes Himself available to all of us, even beggars—no, especially beggars—when we are hungry for Him.

WHAT ARE YOU HUNGRY FOR?

Are you as desperate to get into God's presence and hear the Master speak as Zacchaeus and Bartimaeus were? God says you will find Him if you look for Him with all your heart and soul (Deuteronomy 4:29). That means our relationship with Him has to be our consuming passion. Here are a couple of heart tests that will help you discover what you're hungry for.

First, ask an honest friend. The Spanish have a saying: "When people are hungry, they talk about bread." Your friends will know what's most important to you by what you talk about.

Experiencing the manifest presence of God doesn't satisfy your hunger; it only whets your appetite for more.

One day a woman told me she had just met a guy she really liked. They hadn't met face-to-face yet, but they'd been talking on the phone for about a month.

"How's his relationship with the Lord?" I asked.

"We haven't gotten there yet," she replied.

"Let me tell you something," I said. "If stuff about his relationship with God didn't come pouring out of his mouth in the first fifteen minutes of your very first conversation, it means it's not his consuming passion."

When your heart is hungry for God's presence, you'll talk about the Bread of Life.

Second, ask yourself this question: What keeps me awake at night? If worries about money keep you awake, maybe you're materialistic. If worries about your job keep you awake, maybe you're a workaholic. But if thoughts of God keep you awake at night, it's probably because hunger for God's presence is your driving passion.

Experiencing the manifest presence of God doesn't satisfy your hunger; it only whets your appetite for more. That was Paul's story. He was consumed with a desire to get close to God because he'd experienced the manifest presence of God on the road to Damascus. That's why he said, "I consider everything a loss compared to the surpassing greatness of knowing Christ Jesus my Lord" (Philippians 3:8). Once you taste the manifest presence of God, you're ruined for anything else. You want more.

That's what Moses wanted too.

PLEASE GO WITH ME!

In chapter 2 we talked about how the Israelites lapsed into idolatry while the Lord was meeting with Moses on Mount Sinai to give him the Ten Commandments. In total disregard for the living God who had just delivered them from slavery, they became impatient and built a golden calf and worshiped it (Exodus 32:8).

After God punished the Israelites, He told Moses to continue the journey to the Promised Land and said He would continue to protect and provide for the Hebrews along the way. But then He made this astonishing comment: "Go up to the land flowing with milk and honey. *But I will not go with you, because you are a stiff-necked people and I might destroy you on the way*" (Exodus 33:3).

Can you imagine Moses' distress when God said He was going to withdraw His presence from the Israelites? Moses reminded the Lord that the Hebrews were His chosen people and begged God to reconsider His decision. "If your Presence does not go with us," Moses said, "do not send us up from here" (v. 15). He didn't want the Promised Land without the Presence. As I picture the scene, I can almost hear Moses pleading, "Don't give up on us, Lord! I need You. I trust You. Go with us! Guide me! Meet with me! Speak to me!"

God had faithfully delivered Moses and the Israelites in dramatic fashion. Yet Moses needed God's presence more than God's victory over his enemies, more than his ability to lead the people, more than physical food and water, and more than another miracle. Nothing less would do.

God wants followers as desperate for His presence as Moses was—people who balk at the idea of going anywhere without Him. However, God will remove His presence from stiff-necked people. Although He said that to the Israelites, not much has changed in 3,500 years. Time and again, we prove by our actions that we are not as concerned with being in the presence of God as we are with stubbornly going our own ways. Think about how you feel when you are around a stubborn child. Do you find yourself growing impatient and irritable? Just as we don't enjoy being around brats, I imagine God doesn't want to be around us when we act like self-indulgent children.

If you find you do not hunger for God as a starving man does for bread, evaluate yourself to see if you have become stiff-necked. For an excellent biblical example, we need look no further than the history of the Israelites during their long journey to the Promised Land.

The waves in the Red Sea had hardly subsided after drowning the army of Pharaoh before the Israelites returned to their primary pastime —causing grief to God and Moses. For the next forty years the people grumbled, disobeyed, rebelled, and ultimately dropped dead in the desert. Moses said that people had provoked the Lord so much at Horeb that He had been ready to destroy them (Deuteronomy 9:8). The Lord relented, but this group would not be permitted to enter the Promised Land; this blessing would have to wait for the next generation.

It would really be easy for me to get down on the Israelites—that is, until I start to think of my own lapses into idolatry. I am completely aware of the sacrifice Christ made on my behalf. Yet how many times have I gotten sidetracked building this golden calf or that altar to a self-styled god?

Ask the Lord to forgive any rebellion that keeps you from desperately seeking Him. Ask Him to give you a genuine hunger for Him as you seek to follow His plan for your life. Trust in the promise of His Word: He will respond to those who hunger for Him (Luke 6:21).

When your heart is hungry for God, He will show up, He will speak to you, and He will change your life forever—just as He changed the lives of Ron and Zacchaeus and Bartimaeus.

WHERE ARE YOU NOW?

❖

TAKE TIME FOR A GPS READING:

- How can I know if I'm hungry for God's manifest presence?

- Am I truly desperate for God to show up? If so, am I willing to admit it?

- In what areas of my life am I being stiff-necked right now?

- What idols have I built for myself?

❖ ❖ ❖

Lord Jesus, I'm desperately hungry for Your manifest presence. Right now I call out to You just like a blind beggar. Lord, I need You. Unless You go with me, I won't make it. Without Your presence, I too easily lapse into idolatry and drop in the desert of my circumstances. Father, we thank You that You are willing to meet desperate people where they are, feed them, heal them, and change their lives forever. I ask You to help me remove any barriers that may be keeping me from being in Your presence.

❖ ❖ ❖

FIFTEEN

The Voice Behind You

❖

Whether you turn to the right or to the left,

your ears will hear a voice behind you,

saying, "This is the way, walk in it."

—Isaiah 30:21

❖

After our two-week honeymoon, Jerry and I needed to buy groceries. I thought if we went shopping together, I could impress him. I was going to show him that I was his very own Martha Stewart and save him from the barbaric state of bachelorhood.

We walked down the water aisle first, and he looked at me and asked, "Sweetheart, darling, precious, what type of water would you prefer?"

I said, "Uh, the cheap kind." I mean, water is water, isn't it?

Jerry explained why one kind was better than another. He knew all about it because he had tried several kinds of water and knew which was best.

"All right, baby," I said. "Just pick some water."

Next we went down the aisle with the bathroom and kitchen cleaners, and he asked me which I preferred.

"Um, 409 cleans everything, doesn't it?" I replied.

He explained why one cleaner was better than another. Aisle after aisle it was the same thing. Jerry had tried many products and knew which were best. By the time we finished, I was at the point of tears. The man I'd married knew more about shopping than I did!

In fact, I quickly found out that all my efforts to impress him with my domestic skills were in vain. He was grateful for my hard work, but what he wanted more than anything was a relationship. He desired intimacy with me. He didn't want me to spend my time impressing him; he just wanted me to be close to him.

Our desire shouldn't be to impress God, but to have a relationship with Him.

That's God's desire as well. "He is a God who is passionate about his relationship with you" (Exodus 34:14 NLT). Listen to Him call: "Come near to God and he will come near to you" (James 4:8). Can't you hear the longing in His voice?

In the same way, our desire shouldn't be to impress God, but to have a relationship with Him. That's how we get close to Him and learn to recognize His voice. When my husband calls me on the phone, I don't have to ask who's calling. Because of my relationship with him, I know who it is by the sound of his voice.

So it is with the Lord. Our ability to recognize God's voice hinges on having an intimate relationship with Him. When you have a sold-out hunger for God, you will yearn for His direction, and He will give it. But you must be able to recognize His voice when He speaks to you.

THE SOUND OF HIS VOICE

My family has our own secret language. A certain expression, tone of voice, or choice of words delivers very specific messages to my parents and siblings that no one else would know. We've tried to make others hip to our inside jokes, but so far it hasn't worked. No one knows our secret language but us. We've known one another for so long and in such intimate ways that we speak to one another in a way people outside the family can't understand.

So it is with sheep. They have a secret language with their shepherd that only they understand. In Jesus' day, flocks of different shepherds would spend the night together in the same sheepfold. In the morning when the shepherds came to get their flocks, each shepherd would enter the sheepfold and call his sheep. All of the sheep would hear the call, but only his sheep would recognize his voice, understand the meaning of his call, and follow him. In order to recognize their shepherd's voice, they had to be *his* sheep.

Christians are the Lord's sheep. He is our Shepherd. As we grow in the Lord, we begin to learn how to recognize His voice and understand His messages. A lamb is less capable of distinguishing His shepherd's voice than a sheep is. Lambs learn as they get to know their shepherd and practice responding to his voice. This skill comes over time as the two build a relationship.

Recently I spoke with a friend of mine who works with sheep. He told me that his sheep don't recognize his voice because he doesn't spend enough individual time with them. The art of teaching a sheep to recognize his shepherd's voice is a lost one. With the availability of modern technology, shepherds don't have to spend individual time with the livestock. This keeps intimacy from developing and the sheep from getting to know their owner's voice.

Thankfully, changing times haven't diminished our Shepherd's desire to get to know us. He still wants to be intimately involved with us and speak to us on an individual basis. As you get to know Him, you'll develop your own secret language with Him. The more you get to know Him by spending one-on-one time with Him, the closer you'll get to Him, and the better able you will be to recognize His voice.

Did you know that a shepherd can stand before his entire flock but call one sheep out at a time simply by the tone of voice he uses? If he and the sheep have spent enough time together, the two have a language that is uniquely theirs.

When God calls us, He calls us personally, by name, just as He did Samuel. There can be no greater blessing than to have a relationship with the Good Shepherd in which we know when He is specifically calling us. When we get into an intimate relationship with Him through His Word, we become acquainted with His character, language, and tone of voice. This enables us to recognize His voice and, by the power of the Holy Spirit, to discern the voices of strangers (John 10:5).

My Plans—or His?

Sometimes God interrupts us to give us His direction. I am learning to recognize my Shepherd's voice in interruptions, but for a long time I often became frustrated when God tried to change my direction so my plans would coincide with His.

I find interruptions particularly irritating when I'm focused on getting an item crossed off my to-do list. I don't want anyone or anything getting in the way of my schedule. But more and more the Lord is showing me that what I consider interruptions are often His way of revealing His plans for me.

As I write, Jackson tugs on my pants leg, calling "Mommy!" and trying desperately to get my attention. My first inclination is to shoo him away and get back to work, but the Holy Spirit reminds me that Jackson is not an interruption. He is my first ministry! Ignoring what seems like an interruption ignores God's attempt to move me away from my plan for my day to *His* plan for my day.

Isaiah gives us a basic principle for life. He tells us that God's thoughts are not our thoughts and our ways are not His ways (Isaiah 55:8). When I read this verse, I'm reminded of all the times that life's busyness has blinded me to what God had for me. God sees the big picture. He is in control. Sister, to continue with your plans without regarding life's interruptions is to ignore God's leading and voice. When we desire God's best for us but become annoyed when He steps in to change the course of our lives, we refuse to accept the very thing we prayed for.

When I graduated from college with a degree in communications, I wanted to work in television. Though I tried to get into the business, my phone calls weren't returned, my résumé wasn't reviewed, and all my efforts fell flat. Even the few television shows I was hired to work on were cancelled shortly after I arrived. All of these problems were major interruptions in my plans. But instead of seeing them as God's divine intervention to reveal His direction for me, I rebelliously kept trying to forge my own path. Can you relate?

A wise pastor said something that changed my perspective: "Priscilla, God interrupted your plans on other occasions. If He used those interruptions to guide you to His will, He can and will interrupt anything that goes against His plans for you now. Your job is to be hungry enough to receive His direction. He will reveal it to you."

What a freeing thought for me!

Think about the Israelites, trudging across the desert, grumbling and complaining as they traveled. They brought immense suffering on their heads because they trusted their own plans instead of God's. They would not have gone through much of what they did had they aligned themselves with Him.

Why are we so often willing to pay the high price of doing our own thing when following God's advice is far less costly and energy consuming? Like the Jews, we are often willing to travel through dangerous territory simply because we want to follow our own direction instead of consulting God. Can you commit to trusting in God's direction even when it seems contrary to what you want or think you need?

> *It's God's job to cause you*
> *to want to do what is right* and
> *give you the power to pull it off.*

Scripture says the "Lord longs to be gracious to you . . . He waits on high to have compassion on you" (Isaiah 30:18 NASB). That message applies to us! God will listen and respond when we go to Him for guidance. When we do, our ears will hear a voice behind us, saying, "This is the way; walk in it" (Isaiah 30:21).

SPIRITUAL TASTE BUDS

Receiving God's direction and following it are two different things. What if I don't *want* to walk in the way He says to go? I've often claimed to desire God's direction for my life, but what I've really wanted is for Him to bless the path I've already chosen for myself. How can I follow God's direction when my heart's not really in it?

Paul gives you a bit of truth you need to know: "God is working in you, giving you the desire to obey him and the power to do what pleases him" (Philippians 2:13 NLT). This remarkable verse says that desiring and doing God's will are not our responsibility; they are His. In other words, it's God's job to cause you to want to do what is right *and* give you the power to pull it off. What a relief, huh?

When I was pregnant with my first son, I began a love affair with chocolate. I never really had a taste for it until my eighth month of pregnancy. Then one day, all of a sudden I wanted chocolate. Something happened while the new life was growing inside me that completely changed my taste buds and made me desire something I had never wanted before. Now I can't seem to get enough of it.

When the new life of the Holy Spirit takes up residence in you, He begins to change your spiritual taste buds. He causes you to understand and desire God's will for you. This means that when you and I are in fellowship with God and remain in His Word, our emotions and understanding will change so that we desire the same things God desires.

No longer do I frantically search for God's will; now I just desperately search for God. I trust that it is His responsibility to show me what He wants me to do and how I am to go about doing it. As I seek Him, stay in His Word, and confess my sins, He transforms my mind and emotions to align with His plans and purposes for my life.

I still love chocolate. At least two or three times a week, I indulge myself and nibble on something that has chocolate in it. It's still unbelievable to me that my tastes changed so radically because of my pregnancy, but that's what happens when new life takes up residence in you. When the Holy Spirit takes up residence in us, He changes our tastes more and more every day so that we desire to do what pleases Him.

THIS IS THE WAY

In 1 John 2:4 the term "know" means *to know intimately.* To know God in this sense is not to just have a casual relationship with Him but to know details about Him in a way that is special and specific to just the two of you. John says that the test for determining whether or not we truly know the Lord is if we keep His commandments (1 John 2:3–6).

Jesus makes this stunning promise: "'He who has My commandments and keeps them is the one who loves Me; and he who loves Me will be loved by My Father, and *I will love him and will disclose Myself to him*'" (John 14:21 NASB). Surely this is one of the great promises of Scripture! Jesus gives us the key to hearing His voice: grow in intimacy with Him and obey His Word.

Obedience is the key that opens the door to hearing God's still, small voice. If we want to keep the lines of communication open and flourishing between God and us, we must commit to obey Him.

The closer we are to God, the more readily we will hear His voice.

I am certain that Satan wants us to miss the importance of intimacy with the Lord. He wants us to be so busy trying to impress God that we miss out on the closeness He desires. The Enemy does this because he knows that an intimate relationship with God is where we experience His presence and power.

God is too great to be impressed by all our activity. People might be impressed, but God won't be. We bring a smile to His face when we sit at His feet, hear His voice, and discover the secrets reserved for His friends. May we respond to the Lord as David did: "My heart has heard you say, 'Come and talk with me.' And my heart responds, 'Lord, I am coming'" (Psalm 27:8 NLT).

WHERE ARE YOU NOW?

❖

TAKE TIME FOR A GPS READING:

• Have I spent enough one-on-one time with God to enable me to recognize His voice?

• How do I respond when my plans are interrupted?

• Can I name some specific decisions I've made that show others I truly know the Lord?

• Do I seek God's direction, or do I seek His blessing on my own direction?

❖ ❖ ❖

*Heavenly Father, thank You that You feed all who hunger
for Your power, Your presence, and Your direction.
I confess that instead of wanting an intimate relationship
with You, I often just want to impress You or others.
Forgive me, Lord. I want to hear You call me by name.
When You say, "Come talk with Me,"
may I always respond, "Lord, I'm coming."*

❖ ❖ ❖

PART SIX

A Servant Spirit

Speak, for *Your servant* is listening.

—1 Samuel 3:10 NASB

❖

The final characteristic that we find to be true of Samuel is that he was a servant. Samuel called himself a *bondman*—someone who had chosen to be a servant and willingly submit to someone else. God had gifted Samuel to be a prophet, and Samuel submitted to God's call on his life, even though it meant putting his feelings aside and accepting difficult tasks. Samuel was able to do those things because he had the spirit of a servant.

*Gifted
to Serve*

❖

*Each one should use whatever gift he has received
to serve others, faithfully administering God's
grace in its various forms.*

—1 Peter 4:10

❖

She was fifteen years old when she gave her life to the Lord. While visiting a Christian camp, she told the Lord she was committed to being His servant—with one exception. She didn't want to be a pastor's wife.

Three years later at a revival she met the man who would be her husband. Their life together took them through Bible college and seminary. She was excited about their life of ministry together—until the day her husband announced that God was calling him to be a pastor. This was the one thing she didn't want to do with her life. It took her two years to accept and yield to God's plan for her.

> *Genuine happiness comes from*
> *fulfilling God's purpose for us.*

My mother, Lois Evans, has now been a pastor's wife for more than thirty years. She and my father, Tony, have ministered faithfully to a congregation that has grown from ten people to more than seven thousand. Now she realizes this is what God had in mind all along.

CALLED TO SERVE

No matter what our profession, as Christians we are called to serve in God's kingdom. God doesn't arbitrarily demand that we serve Him. He doesn't force us to work because He needs servants. After all, He created the universe from nothing with a word. He can do anything He wants quite nicely, thank you. God commands us to serve Him because, as our Maker, He knows what will bring us fulfillment.

Write the following statement on your mind in forty-point type: Genuine happiness comes from fulfilling God's purpose for us. Finding and serving in your calling results in a sense of purpose, spiritual growth, and a feeling of satisfaction that you can get in no other way. When you submit to God's assignment, you find true peace and contentment.

Submitting to God's purposes is also a great privilege. I love to think of our personal callings as invitations to be part of something divine. When I'm invited to a friend's house for dinner or a party, I don't go over and try to run things. I don't plan dinner, set the table, invite the guests, clean up the house, or take over the program. As the invitee, my part is simply to show up, go with the flow, and enjoy the festivities.

God has invited us to be part of something great. Our duty is to participate in what He has planned. Scripture says, "And we know that in all things God works for the good of those who love him, who have been called according to his purpose" (Romans 8:28). With this in mind, let's decide to willingly go along with God's plans instead of insisting on our own. The Lord does not and will not make us do anything. He will invite us, and we will be blessed as we submit to His calling on our lives.

> *A quick look at how you submit*
> *to earthly authority will indicate*
> *how you submit to divine authority.*

A true servant of God must be willing to surrender completely to God's plan. Submission is the heart of servanthood. It means yielding to the authority of another. If you and I want to be the kind of servants God can use, we have to check our submission level. A quick look at how you submit to earthly authority will indicate how you submit to divine authority. What does your level of submission to your spouse, boss, or government reveal about you?

Think about how Samuel submitted to Eli. Three times he thought Eli was calling. Three times he got up out of his warm bed and ran into the other room to see if his mentor needed his help. I don't know about you, but after Eli denied having called for the second time, I would have thought his senility was kicking in and wouldn't have answered the next time he called. But three times Samuel willingly submitted to Eli's authority.

SET UP TO SERVE

We must also understand that we have been set up to serve. God created us for a specific purpose. He made us "to do good works, which God prepared in advance for us to do" (Ephesians 2:10). He says that before we were even conceived, we were on His mind:

"Before I formed you in the womb I knew you, before you were born I set you apart" (Jeremiah 1:5).

My sister, you are not in your family, your neighborhood, or your job by accident. God planned everything and created you with exactly what you need to complete the tasks He has for you while you're here on earth. To walk in His plan you must simply present yourself to Him as a servant.

God not only set you aside for a specific purpose when He created you; when He re-created you, He also gifted you for service. The Bible says that there are different kinds of spiritual gifts for different kinds of service (1 Corinthians 12:4). The Holy Spirit distributes these gifts to believers depending on what God has called them to do. We can have confidence in submitting to God's assignments when we discover our gifts—our specific abilities to bless the kingdom of God. Actively using our gifts for God's glory fulfills our callings.

No Self-Service

The very word *gift* implies that we neither select nor deserve God's spiritual gifts. They are an extension of God's grace, delightful treasures we are to enjoy and invest back into His kingdom. Sometimes, however, we use our gifts for personal reward instead of for serving God.

When I first began speaking, I learned that motivational speakers are in high demand. As one of two female speakers with the Zig Ziglar Corporation and the only African-American speaker, I was a highly requested presenter. I was paid top dollar to speak to audiences in a corporate setting. But after several years of traveling as a motivational speaker, I sensed growing personal dissatisfaction. I closed seminars feeling unfulfilled. I wanted to do more than make an audience laugh— I wanted their lives to be changed. My bank account grew larger, but my spirit grew less satisfied.

I asked the Lord about those feelings, wondering what I was doing wrong. Perhaps I wasn't meant to speak. Dozens of scenarios flew through my mind, leaving me empty and discouraged. Then one day the

Lord spoke to my heart. He affirmed that He'd given me the gift of teaching but pointed out that I was using the talent for my own benefit rather than for His kingdom.

Over the next months I discovered that with each corporate speaking engagement I accepted, the Holy Spirit tugged at my thoughts: *Stop riding your own dreams, Priscilla. Ride the tide of My plan for you.*

As I struggled to give up my will and obey His leading, God continued to speak to me through Scripture, patiently bending me to His purposes by revealing His perspective. My heart transition began when I read 2 Corinthians 4:18: "We fix our eyes not on what is seen, but on what is unseen. For what is seen is temporary, but what is unseen is eternal."

Paul's life ambition was to please God because he understood that the things of this world are only temporary. Instead of focusing his attention on earthly things, Paul fixed his eyes on things that are eternal. This was a powerful reminder to me of why God had given me specific gifts! They were to fulfill assignments that have eternal results. I simply needed to put them to work serving God.

According to 2 Corinthians 5:20, the role of an ambassador is to reconcile people to God. As my eyes scanned that verse, I realized I'd become an ambassador of Priscilla instead of an ambassador of the Lord. Making money had become more important to me than being a part of the eternal purpose God had for my life.

Nothing is wrong with making money. Nothing is wrong with having a nice house and a new car. Those things, however, are temporary. You and I are here for more than the temporary happiness earthly things provide. When you understand and accept your God-given assignment, begin to utilize your gifts to fulfill it, and present yourself to God as a servant just like Samuel did, you will find divine satisfaction—a contentment this world cannot provide.

THE GREEN-EYED MONSTER

To discover our unique gifts and use them to carry out the assignments God has for us to do, we must slay the green-eyed monster of envy. Christian women often envy another's gifts, talents, and abilities. Oftentimes we spend so much time wanting to be someone else or have her gifts that we never get around to being ourselves or using what God has given us. If you're busy trying to play somebody else on the stage of life, who in the world is going to play *you*?

The apostle Paul says: "I urge you, [sisters], in view of God's mercy, to offer your bodies as living sacrifices, holy and pleasing to God—this is your spiritual act of worship" (Romans 12:1). Did you catch that? Paul says to offer *your* body.

If we would spend half the energy offering ourselves to God as we do comparing ourselves with somebody else, how much more would we be able to accomplish for Him? One of the best things you can do to serve God is to simply accept who you are. On the day he heard God's voice, Samuel wasn't concerned with what the people around him were doing, and you shouldn't be concerned either. He was offering himself and his gifts to God as a willing servant. Your abilities come from God. Dedicate them to His glory no matter what they are.

ALL IN GOOD TIME

The question at the heart of this book, the question I've asked God over and over, is "What must I do to put myself in a position to hear from You?" And again and again I've had to confront the reality that, while I can put myself in a position to hear from God so that I am ready when He calls, I cannot *make* Him speak. Of all the things God has asked of me as I've sought to present myself to Him as a servant, this has been the hardest: doing nothing as I wait to hear from Him.

The prophet Habakkuk lived at a time when the Israelites' enemies threatened to overwhelm them, and he couldn't understand how God could allow this to happen to His people. Habakkuk cried out for help and eagerly waited for God's response. The prophet was so anxious to hear from God that he compared himself to a guard stationed on a watchtower: "I will stand on my guard post and station myself on the rampart; and I will keep watch to see what He will speak to me" (Habakkuk 2:1 NASB). Habakkuk longed to hear God's voice, and he was determined to wait for God's response. How would you describe your stance as you await God's fresh words for you?

I want to be like Habakkuk as I wait to hear from God. But I'm impatient. Waiting isn't one of my strong suits. Whether I'm hungry and waiting on a meal, sitting in an airplane terminal waiting on a delayed flight, or waiting on God to make good on a promise, I hate delays. Yet God often waits to speak to us, for He says, "The revelation awaits an appointed time" (v. 3). Waiting is very much a part of presenting yourself to God as a true servant.

The Hebrew word for "appointed time" means *sacred season,* or a time set aside for a special spiritual event. Something that is sacred is set apart to bring God glory. Therefore, not only the events, but also the seasons in which they occur bring Him glory. We mustn't attempt to rush God. Rushing spoils the very reason God plans the event for us and cheats us of the joy that comes when we finally experience it.

Not long ago, Jerry was planning a surprise date. He told me that it was going to take place, but he didn't tell me when or give me any details. Being impatient, I kept interfering with his plans by asking questions and making suggestions. The more answers I demanded, the more certain I became that Jerry was incapable of planning a big, fancy date without my help. At least that's how it seemed to Jerry.

By the time the date night actually arrived, neither Jerry nor I felt excited about the event. The joy was gone. I'd worked so hard to make sure Jerry did everything "right" that I was exhausted. Worse, my impatience had ruined a beautiful evening. God's sacred seasons for our lives can be like the date Jerry planned. God sometimes gives us pieces of information about what may occur, but in our eagerness to see it come to pass, we rush the plans and try to tweak them to fit our desires and goals.

The root issue here is a lack of trust that leads us to try to take charge of the situation. Our lack of patience indicates we don't really believe the God we claim to trust. The psalmist proclaims, "With all my heart, I am waiting, Lord, for you! I trust your promises" (Psalm 130:5 CEV). Ask the Lord to help you, through the power of the Holy Spirit, to remain patient as you seek to hear from Him.

Godly service means laying aside our desires and submitting to His, whatever the task and whatever the timing. When we do this, we prepare ourselves to hear clearly from Him when He chooses to speak.

WHERE ARE YOU NOW?

❖

TAKE TIME FOR A GPS READING:

• If someone were to ask me what my spiritual gifts are, what would I say?

• Which gifts do I envy because I think they are so much greater than mine?

• Where have I invested my talents?

• What is my attitude about continuing to serve when God is silent?

❖ ❖ ❖

Father, I am so thankful that You gave my life meaning by planning good works for me to do even before You created me. And thank You that when I was born again, You gifted me to serve in ways that only I can. Help me keep my eyes off what others are doing so I can focus on what You are doing through me. I lay my gifts on Your altar instead of on the altar of my own ambition.

❖ ❖ ❖

Sacrificial Offerings

❖

Sacrifices and offerings, burnt offerings

and sin offerings you did not desire,

nor were you pleased with them. . . .

Here I am, I have come to do your will.

—Hebrews 10:8–9

❖

One day as Jerry, Jackson, and I flew home from a trip to Atlanta, I felt overwhelmed and frustrated. After waking up early to get everybody to the airport on time, I was exhausted. My second pregnancy made me feel perpetually tired.

My exhaustion didn't matter to my son, who ran excitedly through the airport in search of fun. When we boarded the plane, he was even more excited. He played and laughed with the people sitting in front of and behind him, so I had to stay alert every minute of the one-hour delay and two-hour flight.

Once we got home, dinner needed to be made, clothes needed to be washed, and Jackson needed to be bathed. When I finally landed in bed, I wondered: *How did I get myself into this?* But as my head hit the pillow, the Lord reminded me that my family is my first ministry—my divine assignment. Caring for them fulfills part of God's call on my life.

To present ourselves to God as a true servant as Samuel did, we must accept the fact that His assignments don't come free of challenges. Multiple demands often leave us feeling as if we have more than we can handle. Tough times can either derail us from our mission or make us stronger and more committed to following through with what God asks of us. The key to persevering is to make the kinds of sacrificial offerings that enable us to keep doing God's will.

PLACE YOUR FEELINGS ON THE ALTAR

You can be sure that when you serve God, He will sometimes ask you to do things that will make you feel things you don't want to feel. True servants put their feelings aside and focus on doing what God asks them to do.

When God's Message Makes You Feel Afraid

When Samuel heard the Lord calling, his response was, "Speak, LORD, for your servant is listening" (1 Samuel 3:9). He presented himself in complete humility and implied that no matter what God asked him to do, he was willing to oblige. Only his servant spirit enabled him to handle what was in store for him.

Remember that God had asked Samuel to tell Eli that his two sons were about to die? Can you imagine how Samuel felt early the next morning when Eli asked him to tell him everything God had said? After all, Eli had mentored him for nine years.

First Samuel 3:15 tells us exactly how Samuel felt. He felt afraid.

Despite his fear, Samuel told Eli everything. He didn't tell him just part of the message or try to sugarcoat it. I love that he did exactly what the Lord told him to do precisely the way he was told to do it. That is the mark of a true servant.

When God's Message Makes You Feel Sad

Jerry and I have some friends named Neal and Sue. They run a conference ministry called Upland's Reach in the Blue Ridge Mountains of North Carolina. They minister to young people and adults year-round, sharing with them the truths of Scripture. One of the arms of their ministry is a camp for young people, and the house they live in is on the camp property.

Recently, Neal and Sue hired a man to help facilitate the campgrounds. He and his family would have to make a long-distance move to help with the ministry, and they had to figure out where they were going to live. As they were trying to work all that out, Sue was sure she heard the Lord tell her that she and Neal should give up their house so the man and his family could live there. With tears streaming down her face at the prospect of leaving the home that she loved, she wrote to me. This is what she said:

> I struggled with this decision for about a month. I didn't want to think about it because even though our home is just an average North Carolina house, it's the only house we've lived in without wheels under it since our marriage twenty-four years ago. I couldn't believe it when the Lord provided it for us. The camp owns the house, but we have been privileged to live in it, and it has served us well. I love this house! It is where our kids have been raised and is all they know.
>
> I can hardly type right now because the tears are streaming down my face, but *I know without a shadow of a doubt that God told me to do this.* When I shared this with Neal, he didn't even seem shocked because he too knew that it was God's will. I'm not sure what the Lord has in

store for us, but I'm willing to do whatever He says. We moved here by faith eighteen years ago in an Airstream travel trailer knowing that the Lord was going to take care of us, and He did. My desire is to build another home right here on camp property, but it would have to be a God-thing because there are no funds to do so. I know He'll come through; I'm just not sure how.

Like Samuel, Sue is a servant who is willing to do whatever God asks, regardless of the way she feels about it.

God told Abraham to offer up his son. He told Hosea to marry a prostitute. He told the disciples to leave everything behind and follow after Him. He told a rich young ruler to give away all his possessions if he wanted eternal life. God the Father told His Son to leave eternity and shed His blood for you and me.

How would it change your attitude if you focused not on what you are giving up but on what you are gaining through obedience?

Be prepared. God may well instruct you to do something that will be hard for you to bear. He may tell you, as He told my friend Sue, to give up your home. He may tell you to take care of your aging parents with no help from your siblings. He may tell you to stay in a marriage with an emotionally detached spouse or in a lower-paying job when a better one presents itself. Whatever He tells you to do, if you have a servant spirit, you will set aside your feelings and do it.

OFFER THE SACRIFICE OF OBEDIENCE

Samuel tells us what delights God. "'Does the LORD delight in burnt offerings and sacrifices as much as in obeying the voice of the

LORD? To obey is better than sacrifice, and to heed is better than the fat of rams'" (1 Samuel 15:22). God expresses the same idea through Jeremiah, "'Obey me, and I will be your God and you will be my people. Walk in all the ways I command you, that it may go well with you'" (Jeremiah 7:23).

Don't mistake what God is saying about obedience. This is no endorsement of works righteousness. We stand before God only on the basis of the imputed righteousness of Christ. But practical obedience grounded in love and gratitude is essential in serving God.

Think about what sacrifices you are currently making in obedience to the Lord. How would it change your attitude if you focused not on what you are giving up but on what you are gaining through obedience? Our adversary gains great traction in our lives whenever he can keep us focused on the imagined costs of obedience. Scripture is filled with examples of those who suffered short-term pain from sacrificial service only to reap long-term gain. Consider some of the examples in the Bible.

Strenuous Obedience

In obedience, Abraham agreed to sacrifice his only son (Genesis 22:1–3). Although God's command turned out to be just a heart test, imagine the agony Abraham suffered.

In obedience, Joseph went to jail because he refused to commit adultery (Genesis 39:10–20).

When Shadrach, Meshach, and Abednego refused to obey the king's demand to worship an idol, they were thrown into a fiery furnace (Daniel 3:14–19).

Peter and the apostles went to jail for preaching Christ. An angel freed them from their prison cell, but they were arrested again, and the religious leaders had them flogged for their faithfulness to God (Acts 5:17–29, 40).

Such obedience is never easy, but it is always worth it. We need to drill the truth deep into our being: Obedience to God always brings rewards—not the least of which is increased communication with God. Think about the rewards those people reaped for their faithfulness.

Rest assured that behind every challenge
we will find God orchestrating
the circumstances to build us up
and bring Himself glory.

God gave Abraham children as numerous as the stars in the heavens (Genesis 22:16–18). Joseph eventually became CEO of the land of Egypt (Genesis 39:21; 41:41–42). Daniel's friends came out of the furnace without so much as the smell of smoke on their robes (Daniel 3:27). Peter and the apostles "left the high council rejoicing that God had counted them worthy to suffer dishonor for the name of Jesus" (Acts 5:41 NLT).

And those were just the earthly rewards!

Trials and challenges are inevitable. We must learn to expect them, submit to them, and learn from them. However, rest assured that behind every challenge we will find God orchestrating the circumstances to build us up and bring Himself glory. John 16:33 says that we will experience suffering and trials in this life, but it also says that Jesus has conquered the world. Through the power of His Holy Spirit, we too can triumph over whatever difficulty comes our way as we serve God.

Simple Obedience

Presenting yourself to God means simple obedience. It applies even to instructions about things that may seem to us to be small and insignificant.

One day when Jackson was two, I asked him to clean up his play area. Excited to get up and move on with the rest of his day, he bounded to his feet and quickly put everything in its proper place. As

I watched Jackson clean up his toys, my heart suddenly filled with love, and I had an overwhelming desire to tell him how much I loved him. So when he was finished, I opened my arms to him and said, "Come here, Sweetie." But Jackson didn't want to come to me. In fact, my instruction seemed to repel him. He ran from me!

I marveled that he had easily made the effort to clean up his play area, but he fought against the simple obedience required to come to me. Cleaning up took a lot more work than coming to me, but he didn't obey my simple instructions. *How like our relationship to God!* I thought. We often run from God's simplest requests.

I suspect that most of the time our motives for disobedience are more mixed than the tangle of necklaces in a jewelry box. We can't even begin to figure out why we do what we do. I certainly confess my bewilderment. I don't know why my heart disobeys, but I know it does.

Second Thessalonians 2:7 speaks of the "secret power of lawlessness." This is one verse where I still lean to the King James Version's turn of phrase: "the mystery of iniquity." In light of the obvious fact that everything of value comes from obeying God, and every evil, loss, and destruction comes from disobeying Him, iniquity is truly a mystery. So what do we do about it?

We need to take a personal inventory. We must look into our hearts to see if we are true servants of the Lord. We must dig deep to uncover how we really feel about serving Him. Do we obey the Lord with strings attached? I can't tell you how many times I've told the Lord that I would gladly do what He asked if only He would gladly do for me what I asked. Are we willing to obey God no matter how our assignments make us feel or how difficult they are? Can you and I honestly say, "Speak, Lord, for Your servant is listening," and truly, without reservation, mean it?

By offering God the sacrifices of our feelings and our obedience, we align ourselves with His will, open the door to receive His blessing, and find the strength to persevere in the face of challenges. As we do, we position ourselves to hear His voice.

WHERE ARE YOU NOW?

❖

TAKE TIME FOR A GPS READING:

• What emotions have I had to lay on God's altar in order to serve Him?

• What have been some of God's rewards when I have obeyed Him?

• How do I usually respond when I face challenges in serving God?

• Do I ever bargain with God when He asks me to do something?

❖ ❖ ❖

Father, I have taken inventory of my heart, and I truly want to serve You. I confess that my emotions can get in the way and that sometimes what You ask seems too hard for me to bear and too hard for me to do. But then I picture Your Son on the cross, serving even unto death, and I know that You will never ask me to do anything You have not equipped me to do. Help me persevere as I listen for Your voice.

❖ ❖ ❖

Modeled Servanthood

❖

He got up from the meal, took off his outer

clothing, and wrapped a towel around his waist.

After that, he poured water into a basin

and began to wash his disciples' feet.

—John 13:4–5

❖

 n 1991 I went to Haiti with others from my church to serve in missionary efforts to share the gospel and help construct a dormitory building. I wasn't prepared for what I found there.

I was saddened and even alarmed by the conditions we were asked to live in. Although the missions organization that provided our accommodations tried to make us as comfortable as possible, we still had to use the roach-filled outhouse, take a shower with cold water that came out of the waist-high faucet in a single stream, and sleep in a bunk bed on a hard mattress.

Each morning we would wake up to the sound of children playing. One of those children was nine-year-old Manette. Despite her terrible environment, Manette never stopped smiling. With no real bed to sleep on and no assurance of when she would eat her next meal, Manette still smiled. That smiling little Haitian girl caused an American teenager to take a closer look at herself. And I didn't like what I saw.

When I looked into the mirror of Manette's smile, I remembered every grudging comment I'd made about the beds and showers and outhouses. I remembered how I had complained about the seat I had been given on the plane, the length of the flight to Haiti, and even the shots I had to take to be eligible for the trip. When I looked into the mirror of her smile, I remembered the many times I had frowned because the food wasn't cooked just the way I liked it or the lemonade was too tart. I remembered the times I hadn't thanked the Creator for my meal, but just plunged in instead. I remembered how I had scowled at our accommodations when I saw roaches darting from underneath my bed.

Two of the many lessons Manette taught me were these: Service requires you to step out of your comfort zone, and service is often as simple as doing the mundane things of life with a smile on your face.

THE MODEL SERVANT

Our Savior is the ultimate model of true servanthood. In John 13, we find Jesus in the upper room, seated around the dinner table with His disciples. He knew His hour had come and that He was about to be betrayed. But He couldn't leave that place until He was sure His disciples understood what it meant to be a servant in God's kingdom. So He poured water into a basin and began to wash the disciples' feet, an act that revealed His love for those He was directly serving, His humility, and His submission to God. That night, Jesus modeled how we are to serve Him and others. Verse 4 says He did three things.

Jesus Got Up

The first thing Jesus did was get up from the meal. Verses 12 and 26 tell us that the meal wasn't even finished yet. We know that Jesus was deity, but He was clothed in humanity, and like any man, He liked to eat. To get up from a meal to serve others was a sacrifice. But Jesus made the choice to leave behind His own satisfaction and comfort and to serve His disciples by performing a menial task usually reserved for the lowliest servant. He got up from a tableful of food to wash feet.

It would never occur to me to get up from the table to wash feet. I love to eat, and the meal I like best is dinner. I just love having a satisfying dinner, especially in a nice restaurant with candles on the table and music playing in the background. The problem is that now that I have two kids, I don't enjoy dinners as much. Jackson throws vegetables on the floor; Jerry Jr. pulls meat off my plate; my husband needs a napkin. You know the drill. Meanwhile, as I run around trying to serve everybody, I complain about my interrupted meal with a sour expression on my face. I don't want to serve while I'm trying to eat, and I don't want to get up from a meal to serve others.

But Jesus did.

My Savior left behind much more than a tableful of food to serve. He left the comforts of heaven to come to earth and serve us. He left behind a sinless existence just so He could take on our sin. That night at dinner, the disciples ate while Jesus washed their feet. The next day, they used those feet to run away while Christ hung on a cross at Calvary. What a high price our Savior paid to teach us what it means to be a servant!

Are you willing to get up from the table of your own comfort and serve?

Jesus Removed His Outer Garment

The second thing that Jesus did was to take off His outer garment. With its dangling sleeves, it would have gotten wet and kept Him from serving well, so instead of doing a mediocre job, He took it off.

A woman with a true servant spirit is willing to take off anything that keeps her from serving. Sometimes when I'm dressed up I don't want to play with my children. I don't want their sticky little hands on me. But if I want to really be their momma and serve them, it means I've got to take off the cute outfit and put on something I don't mind getting dirty.

Jesus knew that Judas
was about to betray Him,
but He still washed his feet.

Jesus tells us to take off whatever hinders us from serving Him. Maybe you need to take off your expectations of what you thought your life was going to be like so you can gladly serve your children and aging parents. Maybe you need to take off your love affair with material things so you can serve Him faithfully in ministry. Maybe you need to strip off the need to be compensated, rewarded, or thanked by others when you serve them. Or perhaps you need to get rid of the bitterness over what someone has done to you. Think about it. Jesus knew that Judas was about to betray Him, but He still washed his feet. What gets in your way?

I'll be honest with you. What gets in my way most often is pride, plain old pride. I've noticed that most often I don't serve because I'm just too captivated with myself. If anyone had a reason to be proud, it was Jesus. John 17:6 says Jesus knew that the Father had given all things into His hands. He knew that He was the sole pro-prietor of heaven and earth, the lone mediator between God and man, the great umpire and referee of the universe, and the administrator of the kingdom of God among men. Philippians 2:6 says that He knew all of this, yet He chose to empty Himself and take on the form of a bond servant. While the King of Kings and Lord of Lords was will-ing to empty Himself, we're often so full of ourselves that we just can't serve.

What do you need to take off so you'll be free to do what God has called you to do?

Jesus Girded Himself with a Towel

The third thing that Jesus did was to take up a towel and gird Himself with it. A towel, not a loose garment, was the appropriate tool for the task at hand. After rising from the comfort of His meal and laying aside the garment that would get in His way, Jesus took up the equipment He needed to wash feet.

> *When Jesus chose to teach the disciples a lesson about servanthood, He didn't preach a sermon; He did something.*

Godly servanthood calls for tools that suit the task. When you hear God's voice and He gives you instructions, He also gives you the appropriate tools. First Corinthians 12:7 says that each of us has been given very unique and specific tools to use in our service to others. Maybe the reason you find it so difficult to serve in the capacity you're in right now is because you've been rummaging around in somebody else's toolbox and come up with the wrong tool.

I never thought I'd be in ministry, especially not full-time. But one day I just stopped fighting it. As I tried to decipher God's will for my life, I looked at the tools God had given me. That helped me to understand what He wanted me to do for His glory. If you're trying to discover what God has called you to do, just look at what's in your hand. That's the towel that He's given you to wash the feet of the people He will put in your path.

Please notice that when Jesus chose to teach the disciples a lesson about servanthood, He didn't preach a sermon; He did something. He knew the most effective way to teach them was to show them. Being a servant is not about your talk, it's about your walk.

As God seeks to speak to you, will He find someone who is busy talking about being a servant, or someone who's busy serving?

LOWLY TASKS

Becoming a mom has made me a servant. When Jackson was born, for the first time in my life, I learned what it meant to really need help. Recovering from a C-section, not sleeping through the night, and nursing a hungry man-child every three hours quickly took its toll on me. I needed even more help after Jerry Jr. arrived. I was so grateful that the members of my church brought us prepared meals, that my husband cleaned house, and that my son's godmother hovered nearby, seriously seeking to help in any way she could.

Now that I have experienced being a new mother, I have an entirely different outlook on how to help others. I used to be the kind of friend who would call, offer my best wishes, and say, "If you need anything, please call." Now, let's be honest. How often do any of us actually call someone to come wash and fold our dirty laundry or scrub our floors for us? I must admit that, on occasion, I was counting on that. I said I wanted to help, but sometimes I was really busy and didn't really have the time. In other instances, I had the time, but I hoped I wouldn't be asked to do certain things. I wanted to help—but in the way that I wanted to help at a time that was convenient for me.

Sister, that's not service.

Now I'm more serious about service. In fact, I'm so serious that I rarely tell someone to call me if they need anything. These days, instead of offering, I just show up and do, because, honey, I've been there. I'll clean the toilet, take out the garbage, and mop the floor. I'm willing to do whatever mundane, menial task needs to be done. If we're serious about being real servants for God, let's just *show up* and *do*.

SERVICE WITH A SMILE

As a child, I hated Sundays because of kitchen duty. Every Sunday afternoon, my mother cooked delicious dinners for six family members and inevitable guests. Although the meals were wonderful, I always dreaded them because they meant a lot of work for me when it came time to clean up. As I watched Mom cook, I could only think of what lay in store for me. The dishes seemed never ending, and I hated every minute of washing them. I only did it because I had to, and with every dish I scrubbed, pot I cleaned, and countertop I wiped, I let everybody know how I felt about the job.

Today things are different. Sunday dinner is still at Mom's house. And though the meal still makes for a lot of work, I no longer dread the meal's end. Having my own family has made me appreciate the effort that goes into preparing a nice meal for others. Now I willingly offer to take care of the Sunday dinner dishes out of a sincere thankfulness that stems from my heart.

True servants serve God graciously, thankfully, and with no strings attached. God isn't looking for people who claim to want to do what He asks. He's looking for people who are willing to step out of their comfort zones, take on even the most menial of tasks, and do them with a smile on their face.

Are you willing to be a true servant? Then leave your comfort behind. Take off whatever hinders you, pick up your tools, and get to work. When we make the decision to serve God with the heart of a true servant, our spiritual ears will be opened and we'll be able to hear His voice.

Oh, and don't forget to smile!

WHERE ARE YOU NOW?

❖

TAKE TIME FOR A GPS READING:

• What comforts have I left behind to serve God?

• What hinders me from being the kind of servant God wants me to be?

• What kind of tasks do I balk at doing?

• Do I serve others thankfully and with joy?

❖ ❖ ❖

Father, I confess that sometimes I have a bad attitude
about serving. Often I do it because I have to, not because I
want to. I know that such service is not pleasing to You,
Lord, and I repent. Give me the grace to serve You gra-
ciously. I make a commitment right now to serve You with
all my heart and with all my mind and with all my
strength, no matter how difficult or lowly the task. I bow
at Your feet, awaiting Your command.

❖ ❖ ❖

What's Your Position?

❖

Then the LORD called Samuel.

—1 Samuel 3:4

❖

One of my favorite movies is *Elizabeth*. The scene I remember best is the one in which Elizabeth is talking to a friend when she sees the royal guards coming. She knows exactly why they're coming, and she's terrified. Elizabeth's half sister, Mary, is the Queen of England. Mary doesn't like Elizabeth and does everything in her power to make sure that Elizabeth doesn't ascend to the throne. Finally, she has Elizabeth arrested for something she didn't do.

In the scene where Elizabeth sees the guards coming for her, fear is written all over her face as she looks at her friend. I'll never forget her friend looking back at her and saying, "Elizabeth, remember who you are!" Elizabeth's friend was telling her that it didn't matter what they did to her. It didn't matter if they put her in chains. It didn't matter if they threw her in a pit. It didn't matter if they threw her in a fiery furnace. Elizabeth had royal blood running through her veins.

Sister, I'm so glad you've accompanied me through Scripture as we've studied how to position ourselves to hear God's voice. Now as we come to the end of our journey, I want to remind you of one very important thing—you have royal blood running through your veins! As a Christian, you've been bought with a price, and you belong to God. That makes you a princess, and your Father delights in speaking to His daughters. Sometimes we can feel condemned even though God has forgiven us, and when that happens, we have difficulty hearing God speak. Elizabeth's friend had the solution to this problem: Remember who you are!

Think for a moment about the things you like best about yourself. Would you have difficulty making such a list because you see yourself as just a sinner? Or on the other hand, do you readily list your good qualities because you don't really see yourself as guilty before God? Either of these extremes separates us from God.

It may be that as you've read this book and assessed your position in relation to hearing from God, you've realized that you're not yet in God's family and therefore not in a position to hear from the Father. I have wonderful news for you: God's Son, Jesus, makes us acceptable to God and gives us the right to claim Him as our Father.

Trusting that Christ died for your sins *guarantees* your position with God. We are not made acceptable to God by who we are but by *whose* we are. How thankful I am to live on this side of the cross! Because Jesus shed His blood for us, we are right with God and will live in relationship with Him forever.

If you aren't certain you have received the gift of salvation, I urge you to place your trust in Christ right now. Tell Him you are sorry for your sins and that you want to receive the gift He bought you on the cross. If you want to have royal blood running through your veins, pray this prayer:

> *Lord, I am sorry for the things I've done wrong. I thank*
> *You for dying on the cross for me. I recognize that I am a*
> *sinner in need of a Savior, and I believe that You alone*
> *can save me from the penalty for my sins. Please apply*
> *Your blood to my life right now. From this day on I want*
> *to live my life Your way, by the power of Your Spirit*
> *within me. I invite You to come into my life now and*
> *make me a new person. Thank You, Jesus.*

If this is the first time you've prayed a prayer like this, and you meant it in your heart, let me welcome you to God's family! Your position is now in Christ, and you can begin positioning yourself to hear clearly from your Father.

Now that you're in God's family, I encourage you to read *He Speaks to Me* again. The six characteristics we have studied are precious in the sight of God and can only bring you closer to Him. When we cultivate these traits, we'll grow in intimacy with Him and naturally begin to hear His voice more and more clearly. This is the passion of my heart, and I hope it will become the passion of yours as well.

Dear sister, I pray that you will continue to dive into Scripture for yourself, for it is God's personal gift to you. It has your name on it, and as you unwrap its treasures, the Holy Spirit will reveal what God wants to say to you personally. As you listen, ask God to help you apply what you learn to your life. The more you do this, the more clearly you will hear His voice.

About the Author

$\mathcal{P}$riscilla Shirer is a Bible teacher. She graduated from the University of Houston with a bachelor's degree in communications and from Dallas Theological Seminary with a master's degree in biblical studies.

For more than ten years Priscilla has been a conference speaker for major corporations, organizations, and Christian audiences across the United States and the world. Now in full-time ministry to women, Priscilla focuses on the expository teaching of the Word of God. She wants women to understand the uncompromising truths of Scripture and to be able to apply them to their lives in a practical way by the power of the Holy Spirit.

Priscilla is the author of *A Jewel in His Crown*, *A Jewel in His Crown Journal*, and *And We Are Changed: Transforming Encounters with God*. She is the daughter of pastor, speaker, and well-known author Tony Evans. She is married to her best friend, Jerry. The couple resides in Dallas, Texas, with their sons, Jackson and Jerry Jr.

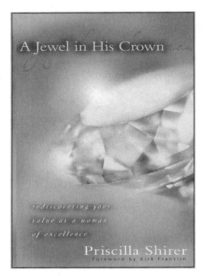

ISBN: 0-8024-4083-5

When they become weary and discouraged, women lose sight of their real value as beloved daughters of God. *A Jewel in His Crown* examines how the way women view their worth deeply affects their relationships. This book teaches women how to renew strength and be women of excellence.

Priscilla Shirer herself is a crown jewel, mined from a family of precious gems. Reading her book is like a walk through Tiffany's as she uses her insight to draw the readers attention to the various facets of a godly woman's character. My prayer is that God will use A Jewel in His Crown *to help women embrace their primary aim of brining glory to God through the uniqueness of who they are in Christ.*

Anne Graham Lotz, AnGel Ministries

A Jewel In His Crown Journal

Rediscovering Your Value As a Woman of Excellence

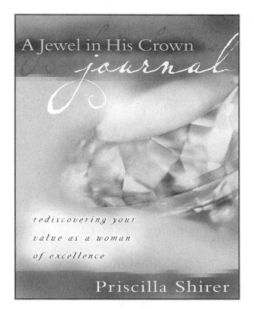

ISBN: 0-8024-4094-0

Did you know that when you became a follower of Christ, you were born into a royal family?

If you have received new life in Christ, then you are a precious daughter of the King of all kings, destined for beauty, holiness, and victory! *A Jewel in His Crown Journal* will lead you through the Scriptures, exploring your inestimable value to God and your identity as His beloved daughter.

This journal is an invaluable tool for all women who want to understand what it means to be a daughter of the King and live their lives as a jewel in His crown.

MOODY
PUBLISHERS
THE NAME YOU CAN TRUST®

1-800-678-6928 www.MoodyPublishers.com

And We Are Changed

Encounters with a Transforming God

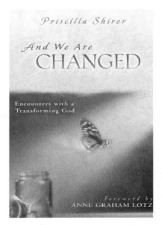

ISBN: 0-8024-3311-1

Have you ever had an encounter with God? Have you come face to face with the Savior? If so, how did you walk away from that experience—exactly the same or forever changed?

When God meets you, His presence, power and love should transform your life—forever! But we often fail to recognize these encounters and allow ourselves to be changed by them. In *And We Are Changed*, Priscilla Shirer shows you what happens when you meet God, the obstacles that keep you from changing, and the ways to experience a miraculous transformation in your life.

If you long to go from complacency and apathy and embrace a life forever changed, this book will show you how. Best-selling author, Liz Curtis Higgs, says, "Priscilla Shirer delivers a powerful, compelling message all women need to hear. Be willing to be changed by a transforming God! *And We Are Changed* combines solid biblical examples and real-life stories that not only move us to tears, they also move us to action. Seedling believer or seasoned saint, if you're ready to partner with God in this business of being made new, *And We Are Changed* has all the encouragement you need to get growing!"

As you apply the principles you have learned in this book and begin to hear God speak to you and move miraculously in your life, I would love to hear your story. Will you share it with me? You can reach me at:

Going Beyond Ministries
P.O. Box 2122
Cedar Hills, Texas 75106-2122
www.gbeyond.com or www.priscillaspeaks.com

248.843

S5582

LINCOLN CHRISTIAN COLLEGE AND SEMINARY

113771

3 4711 00178 3986

W9-CAL-333

3 1668 03603 8

Campfire
Funnies

If you purchased this book without a cover, you should be aware that this book is stolen property. It was reported as "unsold and destroyed" to the publisher, and neither the author nor the publisher has received any payment for this "stripped book."

the TV series SpongeBob SquarePants® created by Stephen

SIMON SPOTLIGHT
An imprint of Simon & Schuster Children's Publishing Division
1230 Avenue of the Americas, New York, New York 10020
© 2006 Viacom International Inc.
All rights reserved.
NICKELODEON, SpongeBob SquarePants, and all related titles, logos, and
including the right of reproduction in whole
or in part in any form.
SIMON SPOTLIGHT and colophon are registered trademarks of
Simon & Schuster, Inc.
Manufactured in the United States of America
First Edition
2 4 6 8 10 9 7 5 3 1
ISBN-13: 978-1-4169-1315-3
ISBN-10: 1-4169-1315-7

NICK

SpongeBob
SquarePants

Campfire
Funnies

by David Lewman

Simon Spotlight/Nickelodeon
New York   London   Toronto   Sydney

FORT WORTH PUBLIC LIBRARY

What does SpongeBob sleep on when he goes camping?

A square mattress.

Why did Plankton smash all the tents?

Because he wanted to break camp.

FORT WORTH PUBLIC LIBRARY

Sandy: What do sheep carry their tents in?

SpongeBob: *Baaaaaackpacks.*

Squidward: What do you get when you cross a bag with an elephant?

Sandy: A *backpachyderm.*

SpongeBob: Why don't tents have any money?

Mr. Krabs: They're always being held up.

Where does Mr. Krabs keep the sticks that hold up his tent?

In a pole vault.

Mr. Krabs: Why will you never go hungry in a tent?

Patrick: Because you'll always have plenty of stakes.

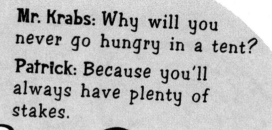

7

SpongeBob: What kind of fire is best for cleaning?

Plankton: A brush fire.

Plankton: Why did the gambler pull up the tent pegs?

Plankton's Computer Wife, Karen: He wanted to raise the stakes.

How did Bubble Buddy like the camping trip?

He was blown away.

Squidward: Was the log entertaining at the wienie roast?

Patrick: Yes, he was on fire.

Why did Patrick throw the candy on the burning log?

He wanted to make a bonbon fire.

Patrick: What do you use to fix a broken fire?

Sandy: A fire drill.

Mr. Krabs: What did the big tent say to the noisy little tent?

Plankton: "Zip it!"

Squidward: What's the secret to opening a tent door?

SpongeBob: You have to know the zip code.

Why is Patrick on a hike like a campfire in the rain?

They're both hard to start.

SpongeBob: What should you carry at night when you're camping underwater?

Sandy: Your splashlight.

Sandy: What did the big camping lantern say to the dark little lantern?

SpongeBob: "Lighten up!"

What does Mr. Krabs carry at night when he's camping?

His cashlight.

SpongeBob: How can you tell when a campfire's sick?

Mrs. Puff: When it doesn't feel so hot.

Mrs. Puff: How did the branch avoid the campfire?

Patrick: He took a stick day.

Sandy: What did the tent think of the campground?

SpongeBob: It was love at first site.

Sandy: Why are lightning bugs always on time?

SpongeBob: Because they're always there in a flash.

Sandy: Did the tent stake have a good date with the rope?

Mr. Krabs: Yes, they decided to tie the knot.

SpongeBob: How did you know Patrick's canteen had a hole in it?

Sandy: It just leaked out.

Patrick: What kind of match is no good for starting a campfire?

SpongeBob: A tennis match.

Squidward: What happened to the log that wouldn't burn?

Plankton: He finally met his match.

17

SpongeBob: What kind of book has no title, no chapters, and no pages?

Sandy: A matchbook.

What happened when SpongeBob left his library book outside the tent overnight?

In the morning it was over-dew.

What happened to SpongeBob's idea for a flying tent?

It never got off the ground.

Squidward: Why did the woodchuck take all the campsites?

Sandy: He was a groundhog.

What does Patrick make by the campfire late at night?

S'nores.

Why did Gary
keep sliding out
of his tent?

He was on his
slipping bag.

Where does Patrick
eat soup when he
goes camping?

In his slurping bag.

Why did Patrick stick warm bread in his sleeping bag?

So his sleeping bag would be nice and toasty.

Squidward: Are hot dogs brave?

Plankton: No, they're wienies.

Squidward: Was the camper mad at his tent when it leaked?

SpongeBob: No, they patched things up.

Why does SpongeBob never take more than two hikes in one day?

Because three hikes and you're out.

Why didn't SpongeBob want to talk about his feet after the hike?

They were a sore subject.

What did Patrick find when he dug under his tent?

He struck soil.

SpongeBob: What's the worst kind of weather for a long hike?

Squidward: Blistery.

23

Why is it so hard for Patrick to sleep if there's a rock under him?

He's used to having the rock *over* him!

Why did Patrick pitch his tent on a boulder?

He wanted to be the new kid on the rock.

SpongeBob: Which campsites are the shiniest?

Patrick: The ones with aluminum soil.

What's SpongeBob's favorite national park?

Yellowstone.

SpongeBob: Is the ground easy to sleep on?

Squidward: No, it's hard.

SpongeBob: What do starfish like to do around a campfire?

Patrick: Have a cling-along.

What kind of camping food does Plankton make at the Chum Bucket?

Beef spew.

SpongeBob: What do jellyfish like to do around a campfire?

Squidward: Have a sting-along.

SpongeBob: Why did the chicken cross the campground?

Patrick: To get to the other site.

Sandy: Why did the fish study camping?

Mrs. Puff: She wanted to join the Girl Trouts.

Patrick: Why did the camper sleep with her head in the grass?

SpongeBob: She wanted to wake up with a new hair dew.

Sandy: What's the difference between the shoes you wear to go camping and two owls on a bicycle?

Squidward: One's a pair of hiking boots and the other's a pair of biking hoots.

SpongeBob: How did the doctor invent a cure for poison ivy?

Sandy: He started from scratch.

Why did Patrick hike through the poison ivy?

He was itching to go.

Why did the bug dig below the tent Patrick's family was in?

He wanted to sleep under the Stars.

Plankton: Who helps campers and keeps the trees in order?

Squidward: The forest arranger.

SpongeBob: Why did the tent agree to stand up all night?

Squidward: He was roped into it.

Plankton: What kind of knot should you never use on a tent rope?

Mrs. Puff: An astronaut.

Squidward: What is the rope expert's motto?

Mr. Krabs: "If at first you don't succeed, tie, tie again."

Patrick: Why did the big knot give the little knot a time-out?

SpongeBob: It was being knotty.

SpongeBob: What do pirates like to camp in?

Patchy the Pirate: An *ahrrrrr-v*.

SpongeBob: Why do pirates go camping?

Patchy the Pirate: To get out and enjoy the fresh *ahrrrrr*.

Plankton: What kind of cot is the worst to sleep on?

Squidward: An apricot.

Sandy: What's huge, lives in a lake, and never remembers to bring a compass?

Squidward: The Lost Ness Monster.

What does Sandy always remember to take when she goes hiking?

Her furs aid kit.

Why did Patrick punch the dirt path?

He heard it was time to hit the trail.

What does the Flying Dutchman sleep on when he goes camping?

A scare mattress.

Sandy: What should you remember to take with you when you hike through the Fairy-Tale Woods?

SpongeBob: An up-to-date troll guide.

SpongeBob: Where did the sloppy camper go hiking?

Sandy: The wildermess.

Squidward: Where did the clumsy camper go hiking?

Plankton: The great ouchdoors.

Patrick: What has long fangs, wears a big cape, and sleeps all day in a tent?
Squidward: A campire.

Why did Patrick tie a leash to the tent?

He heard it was a pup tent.

Pearl: What part of the tent did Cinderella break?

Mrs. Puff: The glass zipper.

Pearl: Why are some musicians especially good at putting up tents?

Squidward: Because they have perfect pitch.

SpongeBob: How did the log feel about being in a campfire?

Squidward: Burned up.

Patrick: What do campfires eat for breakfast?

SpongeBob: Shredded heat.

Plankton: What kind of stick makes the worst kindling?

Pearl: Lipstick.

Squidward: What kind of branch never burns?

Sandy: The branch of a river.

If Squidward were a branch, what kind would he be?

A stick-in-the-mud.

Mermaidman: Where do potatoes like to go camping?

Barnacleboy: In a mashional park.

Mermaidman: Why did the old camper make the young camper crawl around his tent?

Barnacleboy: He wanted to show him the ropes.

What's Mrs. Puff's favorite campfire activity?

Testing marshmallows.

Mr. Krabs: Why are campers never satisfied?
Plankton: Because they always want s'mores.

SpongeBob: What do cows like to make over a campfire?
Sandy: S'moo·rs.

What did SpongeBob tell Patrick when he was searching for the campfire?

"You're getting warmer!"

Why did Patrick just pretend to go on the trail?

He thought Squidward told him to fake a hike.

Squidward: Why did the robbers go camping?

Plankton: They wanted to go on a nice, long heist.

Why did Patrick pitch his tent between a state park and a national park?

He'd always wanted to double-park.

What's the difference between the Patty Wagon and a hiker?

One's got two front seats and the other's got two sore feet.

Patrick: What's every mosquito's favorite bedtime story?

SpongeBob: *Snow Bite and the Seven Pores.*

How did Patrick choose which hot dog to roast?

"Wienie, meeny, miny, mo . . ."

Mr. Krabs: What kind of fire makes the worst campfire?

Squidward: A sapphire.

How does Plankton's computer wife start her day when she's camping?

She boots up.

GOOD NiGHT.